Creative Gardening

Creative Gardening

AURORA PUBLISHING

This edition published in 1995 by
Aurora Publishing
Unit 9, Bradley Fold Trading Estate
Radcliffe Moor Road
Bolton BL2 6RT

Produced by Marshall Cavendish Books, London
(a division of Marshall Cavendish Partworks Ltd)

ISBN 1 85926 060 8

Printed in England

Some of this material has previously appeared in
the Marshall Cavendish partwork *MY GARDEN*

Contents

Introduction

A successful garden is not only an outdoor living area, a place to relax in when the sun comes out. It is also a showpiece which will impress neighbours and visitors and will also provide you with the pleasure of an ever-changing, stunning view from your living room window.

To achieve this, of course, a garden needs style – and style requires planning. Nature, left to its own devices, is more likely to produce a motley collection of unsightly weeds than a chorus of flowers, shrubs and trees in complementary colours and shapes. In planning your garden, the possibilities are virtually limitless. You may want to make it dramatic and colourful, with large beds of bright, open flowers. You may prefer that it is serene and tranquil, perhaps with a pond and small beds of relaxing blues and white flowers showing through in summer. You may want an ordered and formal look or you may prefer the freedom of a wild, untamed appear-ance. In making these decisions it is helpful to remember that thousands have trodden the same path before you. There are several, traditional styles of garden which you might find appealing and wish to emulate in your garden.

The English Cottage Garden came into fashion during the Victorian era. This style of garden is a disorderly mix of colourful flowers and herbs which overflow from their beds onto brick pathways or tiny, daisy-filled lawns. Essential to the cottage garden are large, old-fashioned rose bushes with their rambling appearance and sweet fragrance. These are combined with wild flowers such as foxgloves, along with shrubs and creepers, to give the garden an effect which is at once unruly and shambolic, charming and romantic. One great attraction of the cottage garden is that it requires only a minimum of maintenance.

In sharp contrast to the wild cottage garden, a formal garden uses carefully-defined planting areas, geometrically-shaped paths and beds and delicate, classical ornaments to create an effect which is clean and tidy, with everything in its place. The garden's neat lines are echoed in the

choice of plants, with flowers of subdued pinks and whites planted in rows, offset by neatly-trimmed shrubs and a carefully tended lawn – all combining to create an elegant appearance.

While it developed in warm, sunny climes, the Mediterranean garden can be easily adapted to more temperate locations. The Mediterranean garden offers a unique combination of the formal and the informal – blending square or rectangular beds and pools with straight, gravel or paved pathways and overrunning tubs full of flowers in loud, hot colours. Also characteristic are tall, spiky architectural plants and column-shaped trees such as cypress, which stand out dramatically against a clear, blue sky. The typical Mediterranean garden is also full of the fragrances of fresh herbs such as thyme and rosemary. Typically enclosed with high, whitewashed walls, these gardens act as sun traps and are ideal for outdoor

Introduction *(continued)*

living and, in particular, *al fresco* dining.

Perhaps the most subtle and tranquil of all garden environments is provided by the traditional Oriental garden. Designed to reflect nature as closely as possible, Oriental gardens eskew the harsh angles and lines, along with the bright colours, of many Western gardens. Instead, leafy greens, which are densely planted in small plots, show off their subtly different shades and textures. Ornamentation is provided by still pools and weatherbeaten rocks, creating an effect which is fresh, yet at the same time serene and restful.

There are, of course, more unusual options. You may want to create a bog garden, which – despite its name – will provide a home for all manner of fascinating and colourful plants. You may want to defeat the cycle of the seasons – and keep the time you spend maintaining your garden to a minimum – by planting your garden exclusively or mainly in evergreens (These, despite their name, can be found in a range of colours).

Creative Gardening offers a taste of all these styles and many more. It is designed to help you choose the type of garden which you find most appealing, and to give you ideas from which you can build. Each chapter describes a particular garden style, theme or colour scheme which may suit your garden, outlining which plants to use and how they can be combined in order to achieve a range of effects.

You may want to take two or three traditional styles and use them in different parts of the garden or combine them to create a completely new effect. You may even wish to break all of the rules and come up with something completely new. In creating your dream garden, the possibilities are boundless.

Sunshine and Blue Skies

Imitate the best nature has to offer – fill your garden with harmonious shades of blue and yellow, the brilliant colours of summer.

Blue and yellow form one of the happiest colour combinations in any garden. Blue is reminiscent of summer skies, cool shade and still waters. It has a calming effect and is very restful to the eye, while yellow, the sunshine colour, is warm and cheerful.

Although there are few true blue flowers, there are many delightful shades to choose from – from the palest of sky blues to the richness of royal and cobalt blue.

Yellow comes in countless shades, including cream, soft and bright yellows, buff, ochre, golden and acid yellows.

The two colours can be used together to create some very exciting effects in the garden, but be careful not to base your entire design on sharp contrasts.

Bright splashes

For best effect, most of your garden should be composed of a harmonious blend of hues with just the odd splash of strong, bright colour to catch the eye. Before you get down to planning your blue and yellow garden it is worth spending some time studying the way in which these two colours relate to one another. Browse through books and magazines to see how they are combined in fashion and interior design, or take a stroll through show gardens or a natural landscape, looking out for these colours. You can probably even learn from your neighbours' successes or mistakes.

You may like to carry this

Few colours combine to such stunning effect as blue and yellow. This vibrant forsythia 'Spectabilis' is distinctly defined against a clear blue sky. Colours often mingle with their surroundings but these colours retain their identity perfectly. The yellow exudes life, sunshine and excitement and the blue is tranquil.

PICK OF THE BLUES

Of all the blue-flowered plants available, here are some of the best from which to make your choice.

glory of the snow (*Chionodoxa* species)	winter and spring-flowering bulbs for a sunny position, 15cm/6in high
pansy (*Viola* species)	winter and spring-flowering annuals or biennials for sun or half shade
forget-me-not (*Myosotis* species)	small spring-flowering biennials for either sun or shade
periwinkle (*Vinca* species)	dwarf spring-flowering, evergreen shrubs for sun or shade
California lilac (*Ceanothus* species)	early summer- or autumn-flowering shrubs for a position in full sun
delphiniums	tall summer-flowering perennials that like sun
lobelia (*L. erinus*)	dwarf summer-flowering edging plants for a sunny spot
African lily (*Agapanthus* species)	late summer-flowering perennials, growing to 60cm/2ft high

Golden rod (above) is a hardy perennial with profuse, yellow flowers. Easy to grow, it will quickly give a blast of radiant colour. Blue and yellow in a flower bed can be breathtaking (right). The tulips (Tulipa fosteriana 'Candela') open up their cups to the sun while the grape hyacinth forms a sea of colour.

Blue flowers come in all shapes and sizes. For a showy display choose delphiniums (left). Their towering spikes can be tinged with pink or purple but most stunning of all is the intense pure blue. In contrast, the tiny glory of the snow, Chionodoxa sardensis (below), only grows to 15cm/6in but makes a beautiful addition to any rock garden.

Flowering at the end of the winter, the tiny winter aconite, Eranthis hyemalis (above left), adds the first touch of spring colour to your garden. The chrysanthemum 'Charm' (above right) is very much a summer plant however. Plant it in tubs to display on your patio and you will be able to bring them inside for a yellow colour theme indoors over the winter.

While many blue flowers are small and delicate the Californian lilac, Ceanothus impressus, (below) grows to 3m/10ft. As it is used to warmer climates, grow it in a sheltered spot; against a wall is ideal. Clusters of deep blue flowers appear in spring and remain until early summer.

PICK OF THE YELLOWS

Yellow flowers abound. Here is a selection of shrubs and perennials that are guaranteed to give good value for money.

winter aconite (*Eranthis hyemalis*)	a winter-flowering perennial perfect for a semi-shaded position, 10cm/4in high
witch hazel (*Hamamelis mollis*)	a large, winter-flowering deciduous shrub that thrives in half-shade
gold dust (*Alyssum saxatile*)	a spring-flowering, sun-loving perennial, 30cm/12in high. Thrives in any ordinary well-drained garden soil.
forsythia (*F. × intermedia*)	a group of large, spring-flowering deciduous shrubs that like full sun
shrubby cinquefoil (*Potentilla* species)	small, early summer-flowering deciduous shrubs for sun or half-shade
broom (*Cytisus battandieri*)	a large, summer-flowering semi-evergreen shrub for a sunny spot
evening primrose (*Oenothera* species)	summer-flowering, sun-loving hardy perennials, from 15-120cm/6-48in high
golden rod (*Solidago* species)	late summer-flowering perennials for a sunny spot, 90cm/36in high

11

garden colour scheme into your house – it can be extremely effective. Imagine a room which is decorated in pale yellow and rich shades of blue, opening out into a glorious garden full of delicate yellow snapdragons, marigolds, and day lilies, accented by the towering blue spikes of delphiniums. The effect would be positively stunning!

Select a shade

Once you have an idea of those shades of blue and yellow you would like to use, it is time to select a dominant colour for your scheme. You can either choose one for the whole year or pick a different colour for each season.

In spring, for example, you may like to use lots of bright, cheerful yellows to herald the arrival of a new year. There are plenty of yellow spring flowers to choose from, all of which contrast beautifully with forget-me-nots, scilla and other blue flowers of spring.

Bright blues in summer echo the clear, sunny skies. In autumn, shades of gold, bronze and grey-blues complement the muted, earthy colours typical of this time of year.

Once you have chosen your dominant colour theme for each season, you need to combine each with various other shades of blue and yellow to create a pleasing overall effect.

NATURAL BEAUTY

Blue and yellow flowers abound in natural settings: just think of woods thickly carpeted with bluebells in springtime, and lush green hedgerows dotted with pale yellow primroses.

If you have the space in your garden, why not create your own wildflower patch, using blue and yellow as your theme?
- In a grassy area, blue cornflowers (*Centaurea cyanus*), yellow corn marigolds (*Chrysanthemum segetum*), common toadflax (*Linaria vulgaris*) and meadow buttercups (*Ranunculus acris*) can all be grown from seed, simply scattered in autumn where you want the flowers to appear the following year.
- In a shady, wooded area, the bluebell is really at home. (In fact, the more light it receives, the less intense the colour.) Partner it with yellow archangel (*Lamium galeobdolon*), a dead nettle with bright yellow flower spikes.
- For an area of damp semi-shade, blue bugle is at home with pale yellow primroses, sunny lesser celandine and intense blue germander speedwell (*Veronica chamaedrys*).

A blue and yellow combination often occurs naturally. These hyacinths and tulips form a bright spot in a dull landscape.

These cheerful pansies (right) look gloriously happy when planted in such a wonderful colour combination. The blue makes the lemon yellow seem more vivid while the yellow in turn enhances the purply-blue pansy, drawing attention to the tiny spot of yellow at the centre of its pretty face. They enjoy any fertile, well-drained soil and you can keep them flowering by regularly removing the dead flower-heads.

Blue and yellow can be used to create a wild and unruly effect. The border (left) has been carefully planned to combine blue and yellow plants of varying shades and heights, but the effect is casually charming. Cranesbill (geranium), delphiniums, irises, tall limey-yellow euphorbia and pretty little pansies complete the picture.

Blues and yellows can also be used to create a more simple and formal look (below). Tall, medium and short plants have been planted in military rows but the flowers refuse to be regimented. The deep yellow tickseed, Coreopsis lanceolata, forms a sunny edge. A row of salvia breaks up the blue and yellow, with spikes of stately delphiniums at the back.

The colours you choose should enhance one another rather than detract. For instance, pale yellow and dark blue make a more striking combination than gold and pale blue.

Use soft, muted shades blended together for swathes of soft colour, as well as for softening the effects of strong or bright colours. These will create a warm, restful effect. Be sure to make each patch of subtle colour big enough to hold its own among the splashes of brighter colours.

Dark or strong colours need to be used with care or they will soon overpower your colour scheme. Use them in small amounts as exclamation points in the garden. As a rule of thumb, it is better to let lighter colours dominate darker ones, and weaker colours dominate strong ones.

Soft shades of clear colours

look marvellous massed in large drifts. Misty shades of pastel yellows and blues form an almost dream-like garden setting. You may, on the other hand, prefer to make a bold statement, filling the garden with bright, vibrant colours and contrasts.

Whatever combination of blue and yellow you choose, do not forget to consider the background against which your display will be viewed. Deep green evergreens make a superb background for the various shades of yellow. The paler greens of deciduous shrubs look good behind yellow and blue flowers, but check that their autumn colour does not clash with your colour theme.

Complete harmony

It is also important that your colour scheme should harmonize with its surroundings. Buildings, patios, paths, fences and walls are all part of the final picture, but cannot easily be changed. Garden furniture, pots and containers, however, can be chosen with the blue and yellow colour scheme in mind. Paint fences and gates in a harmonious shade of blue or yellow – or just clean, crisp, brilliant white – to fit in with your theme.

Blue and yellow makes the best use of sun and shade conditions in your garden. Blue will have a cooling effect in a hot, sunny border while yellow can be used to add a splash of colour to a shady area.

INSTANT COLOUR

Fill the spaces in your borders with bedding plants for bright splashes of colour.

For yellows, choose Californian poppies, French and African marigolds and snapdragons, begonias, chrysanthemums and tobacco plants.

For touches of blue, try love-in-a-mist or annual delphiniums.

SHORT CUTS

Summer Colour Schemes

Your garden is an extension of your home, so why not try a little 'exterior decorating'? Start by selecting and co-ordinating a stunning summer colour scheme.

green'. The resulting garden picture may be 'colourful', but at the same time it is quite monotonous. A muddle of colours which pays no attention to change of tone or mood lacks both harmony and interest.

Make a plan

Start by taking a good look at the colours that are already in your garden, including walls, paving, shrubs, trees and the surrounding landscape. This may give you a good starting point for choosing a harmonious scheme of interrelated colours for your flower beds.

Do not feel you must tackle the whole garden at once. Instead, start with a single flower bed and create a colour

O ne of the most exciting aspects of garden design is the way in which colour can be used to create certain moods and feelings. Soft blues and mauves are cool and soothing, yellow is warm and cheerful while reds and oranges are hot and exciting.

Using colour in your garden is a little more tricky than it first seems. Mixed shades of bedding plants and seeds are often planted for a colour 'splash', with no consideration given to how those colours will blend with each other or the surrounding plants.

Plants with purple, gold or variegated foliage are quickly snapped up at the garden centres in the belief that anything is better than 'boring old

A swathe of bright yellow blooms (above) will lift your spirits and bring sunshine into your life even on a dull day. A border filled with bright red flowers, on the other hand, creates a bold and dramatic statement. Red provides a powerful contrast to vivid green leaves in this garden (right). The foliage, which is tinged with crimson, echoes the theme.

co-ordinated design to make it a beautiful, eye-catching summer focal point.

Colour scheming

Look at the colour wheel on the following pages. By choosing flowers from only one of the colour groups you will be able to create a dramatic display in your flower bed. Select shades of blue, for example, or a range of brilliant reds.

This does not mean you are restricted to using a single colour in your scheme. Take your plan one stage further by 'borrowing' plants from the neighbouring colour group and you can introduce contrast without spoiling the overall theme. A few spots of purple or pink in a blue garden, for instance, will greatly enhance the main colour scheme, creating a much more satisfying picture. If you are still not sure how to mix and blend colours, however, choose white as your contrast, and you cannot go far wrong.

Which plant?

Having chosen a colour theme, you are now ready to choose a selection of plants to match. Those with the longest flowering periods keep your scheme going for longer, and save you lots of work too. Foliage plants can make an excellent basic framework for your scheme, especially if the border already contains shrubs.

Green foliage is always useful, as it enhances other plants and can conceal or divert attention when needed. You do not have to stick to green, however, as plants with silver, gold, purple or variegated foliage can be chosen to harmonize with a surrounding colour scheme of, say, yellows, purples or pinks.

While looking through the plant list of your chosen colour scheme, be sure to select those that suit your site and soil conditions. Choose a key plant, then a second to complement the first one and so on, until you` have built up a planting scheme of harmonious colours, textures and shapes. Select each one carefully, considering how it will affect the overall plan. Simplicity and the broad, bold use of colour are the keys to good garden design.

As you arrange and reorganize your plan, you may eliminate some of your original 'key' plants. Keep experimenting until you are happy with the effect. Remember, you are not just selecting plants that will look good side by side, you are creating an overall 'picture'.

Once you are satisfied with your planting scheme, make a

YELLOWS

yarrow (Achillea × 'Moonshine')
lime-yellow lady's mantle
daylily
St John's wort
creamy honeysuckle (Lonicera)
lemon-yellow snapdragons
yellow lilies
golden broom (Cytisus battandieri)
evening primrose
mullein (Verbascum olympicum)
clematis (C. tangutica)
sneezeweed (Helenium)
coneflower (Rudbeckia)
sunny marigolds
yellow-leaved Japanese maple
    (A. japonicum 'Aureum')
golden bamboo (Arundinaria pygmaea
    'Viridistriata')
aucuba (A. japonica 'Gold Splash')
yellow ivies
golden creeping Jenny (Lysimachia
    nummularia 'Aurea')
golden mock orange (Philadelphus
    coronarius 'Aureus')
golden thyme (Thymus citriodorus
    'Aureus')

The golden buttercup-like flowers of St John's wort (Hypericum patulum) provide good bushy ground cover.

Bright yellow flowers and plants with leaves of pale gold create an impact when planted in a large block of 'sunshine' in a mass of green and grey foliage.

The leaves of Acer japonicum 'Aureum' are a light, soft green.

ORANGES

Plants of vivid orange, orange-reds and golden-yellows are the eye-catchers of the border. They give the extrovert gardener a chance to create excitement.

gold dust (Alyssum saxatile)
yarrow (Achillea filipendulina)
pot marigold (Calendula
    officinalis)
geum (G. chiloense)
golden African marigold
yellow-orange coreopsis
    (C. verticullata)
bronze Peruvian lily
daylily
busy Lizzie (Impatiens)

This bright chrysanthemum is called 'Bronze Gertrude'.

red hot poker (Kniphofia)
ligularia (L. dentata)
lily
honeysuckle (Lonicera ×
    brownii 'Fuchsioides')
Iceland and oriental poppies
snapdragon
peony (Paeoni peregrina)
candelabra primula
potentilla
chrysanthemum
montbretia (Crocosmia
    species)
flame-coloured rhododendron
apricot and peach roses

W

Few plants are pure white. Most have a tint of pink, grey, lavender or yellow and should be carefully chosen for a warm or cool theme.

colewort (Crambe
    cordifolia)
thorn (Crataegus x
    lavallei)
deutzia
iris
pink-tinged
    flowering crab
    (Malus species)
sweet cicely
    (Myrrhis
    odorata)
rhododendron
wisteria

REDS

Reds range from dark, purplish tints to brighter orange, and could overpower if used too freely.

peony
poppy (Papaver orientale)
phlox (Phlox subulata)
primula (Primula japonica)
geraniums
pinks, carnations

rhododendron
red roses
petunia
crimson salvia (Salvia
    involucrata)
foxglove (Digitalis purpurea)
cranesbill
daylily (Hemerocallis hybrids
buddleia
colchicum (Colchicum
    speciosum 'Atrorubens')
saffron crocus (Crocus sativu
phlox (Phlox paniculata)
clematis (Clematis sp.)
smoke bush (Cotinus coggyg
    'Royal Purple')

Papaver orientalis (left) is a stunning scarlet poppy – bold and beautiful.

REENS

hemilla (*A. conjuncta*)
man wormwood (*Artemesia pontica*)
lebore (*Helleborus lividus*)
ite variegated dogwood (*Cornus alba* 'Elegantissima')
ite variegated euonymus
in or variegated plantain lily (*Hosta species*)
d nettle (*Lamium*)
ther-of-thousands (*Saxifraga stolonifera*)
iegated weigela (*Weigela florida* 'Variegata')
ne grass (*Elymus arenarius*)
e fescue (*Festuca glauca*)

BLUES

Blues range from deep, inky hues to the palest shades, and have a cool, calming effect.

columbine (*Aquilegia alpina*)
phlox (*Phlox sp.*)
campanula
floss flower (*Ageratum houstonianum*)
Michaelmas daisy
balloon flower (*Platycodon grandiflorum*)
bright blue gentian
blue iris
pale or bright delphiniums
sage (*Salvia azurea*)
monkshood (*Aconitum x cammarum*)
blue African lily
California lilac (*Ceanothus*)
lavender (*Lavandula*)
rose of Sharron (*Hibiscus syriacus*)
blue hydrangea (*Hydrangea macrophylla*)

Tall, stately delphiniums are widely available in a vast range of beautiful blues.

Choose a campanula such as C. aucheri (below) for a garden of purples and blues.

S

amflower (*Tiarella cordifolia*)
ematis
nks (*Dianthus* 'Mrs Sinkins')
by's breath (*Gypsophila paniculata*)
etunia
ses
ichaelmas daisy
hite or cream chrysanthemums
ydrangea
bacco plants
alifornian poppy *Romnega coulteri*;
nemone
eranium
usy Lizzie (*Impatiens*)

PURPLES

Rich purples give strength to a border, while paler mauves have a delicate, old-fashioned charm.

giant bellflower caryopteris (*C. incana*)
bear's breeches (*Acanthus*)
phlox
sedum
sun rose (*Cistus albidus*)
violet-blue *Clematis* 'Lady Betty Balfour'
beauty bush (*Kolkwitzia amabilis*)
lilac (*Syringa sp.*)
fuchsia

abelia (*Abelia x grandiflora*)
mauve hydrangea
Michaelmas daisy
Cupid's dart (*Catananche caerulea*)
cranesbill (*Geranium grandiflorum*)
drumstick primula (*Primula denticulata*)
monkshood (*Aconitum napellus*)
speedwell (*Veronica longifolia*)
pansies and violas
periwinkle (*Vinca major*)
morning glory (*Ipomoea purpurea*)
purple loosestrife (*Lythrum salicaria*)
crocus
autumn crocus (*Colchicum autumnale*)
purple irises

PINKS

Delicate shades of pink create a feeling of peace and harmony, while brighter shades provide vibrant splashes of warm colour.

thrift (*Armeria maritima*)
bellflower (*Campanula punctata*)
pinks, carnations
meadowsweet (*Filipendula palmata*)
tree mallow (*Lavatera maritima*)

Michaelmas daisy (*Aster novi-belgii*)
ornamental onion (*Allium* 'Little Pink Beauty')
cranesbill (*Geranium x* 'Prichard')
geranium (*Pelargonium species*)
petunia
cyclamen
deep pink *Clematis* 'Walter Pennell'

This shocking pink aster (right) would be ideal in a bold pink or mauve colour scheme.

list of your final plant selection. Decide how many plants you will require to fill the designated area and to create a balanced group. To achieve an unstructured look, plant in uneven numbers. When planting perennials, don't forget to take into account their eventual height and spread. Fill any spaces in between with colour co-ordinated annuals so the bed does not look 'gappy'. Be vigilant about self-sown seedlings – nature certainly won't respect your carefully developed colour scheme!

If you want more than one colour theme in your garden and you have several borders to fill, simply repeat the procedure for each area. The borders can be linked by creating a gradient of colour which spills over from one area into the next. The best way to achieve an effect of total harmony in the garden is to select colours once more from the col-

A predominantly pink border (above) includes shades of violet and touches of bright red. Generous splashes of white add brightness, while a good balance of fresh green foliage cools down the overall effect. This island bed (right) is very majestic, with its formal planting scheme and predominance of regal purple highlighted by soft pinks. The theme is further enhanced by a background of cool, dark green foliage and further shades of mauve in the surrounding borders.

our wheel. Instead of selecting individual plants from the adjoining colour sections, choose the predominant colours of the beds from neighbouring sections. For example, one bed could be planted with yellow flowers, its neighbour with

COLOUR CONFIDENT

Q I don't feel very confident about choosing colours. Is there a foolproof formula that guards against error?

A Choose plants with grey-green and silvery foliage to mix in with your flowering plants. The grey leaves will act as 'buffers' between incompatible colours, or link different colour themes. Greys and silvers enhance bright colours and emphasize pale ones, so whatever colour flowers you choose, you can't go wrong.

Look out for some of these plants at your garden centre:

- *Achillea* x *argentea*
- *Achillea* x 'Moonshine'
- *Artemesia* 'Powis Castle'
- *Euonymus fortunei* 'Silver Queen'
- *Euphorbia marginata*
- *Hebe pinguifolia* 'Pagei'
- *Iris pallida dalmatica*
- *Lavendula* species
- *Stachys* species
- *Thymus lanuginosus*
- *Tradescantia fluminentis* 'Alborittata'

Create a stunning and very eye-catching effect by choosing plants from opposite sides of the colour wheel. Orange contrasts wonderfully with bright blue, while sunny yellow and rich purple can look simply sensational. Red roses (right) create brilliant splashes in a sea of greeny-yellow fennel.

Dark green and purple (below right) are cool, calm colours. If you select such a deep and dark colour scheme it is a good idea to include some pale fresh colours for light relief. Here, the paler green leaves of Cornus alba 'Spaethii' create a little pool of light.

shades of orange and flame reds, and a third bed in deep dramatic reds and pinks.

Having carefully chosen and arranged the colours in your garden, the resulting scene will both delight the eye and soothe the soul, and isn't that what a garden is all about? Sit back and await compliments.

Winter Colour

What could be more welcome on a winter's day than a garden aglow with colour? Plan ahead now and you can have plants to please the eye all year round.

When you have spent all spring and summer working away outside to produce a brilliant display that everyone can admire, it is only too easy to forget to plan for the winter months.

A garden that is bare until the first snowdrops appear can be a depressing sight. It is quite possible to have colour in your garden in winter, but this really does need some careful planning. You will have to imagine *now*, before your summer plants have died down, just where a little colour would be most welcome later in the year when the days are shorter and the temperature has plummetted.

Warm indoors

Remember, too, that in winter you will view your garden from the comfort of indoors for most of the time, so you will have to stand at the windows and try to visualize what you will want to see later from inside your home.

Another point to consider is how much space you have. If you have a large garden, it is easy to incorporate areas of winter colour. Smaller spaces can be more difficult to plan: just one patch of late-year colour is not ideal, but you do not want it to be too spread out either, looking as if you are waiting for other plants to emerge in between.

Of course, you do not want anything that requires a lot of attention, or is difficult to find

The aptly named snowflake (right) blooms even in the snow. Its petals are gold-tipped and more rounded than those of the snowdrop.

Use the birch (right) as a specimen tree and its incredible bark will help it to earn a place as one of the most unusual features in the winter garden. When the leaves have dropped the striking colours and texture of the curious bark formation are highlighted.

This garden (below) is bursting with interest and will take on a magical frosted look when temperatures drop. Silver birch, pink and white heathers, red and yellow dogwoods and conifers in all shades of green prove that winter need not be a sleeping season.

Forget the cold and add a touch of the exotic to a winter garden with Fatsia japonica (above). The glossy green leaves are palmate in shape, meaning they look like the palm of a hand, but the plant is also interesting for its white pompom shaped flowers which begin in autumn and last through the winter.

This Viburnum farreri (left) looks like it should be heralding the spring but in fact it begins to flower in late autumn and continues throughout the winter. The deep pink buds burst into clusters of paler, five petalled flowers. They have the added advantage of being richly scented so they fill your senses with delight, cheering you up during the long, dark days.

or expensive to buy. Take advantage of the time you have in the summer months to make your plans, and to visit garden centres to compare prices and choose your plants.

Plant shuffle

Consider the taller plants first and then consider the fronts of borders, any rockeries, containers and window boxes. You may find that you want to move some existing shrubs to

fit in with your new plan, and the best time to do this would be in the autumn, when they are dormant.

Winter jasmine (*Jasminum nudiflorum*) produces profuse bright yellow flowers without the slightest trouble, but this wall plant is often misguidedly pushed into corners and against front doors where it can be admired only by visitors or passers-by. How much better it would be to place it

DECORATIVE BARK

Trees with attractive bark can provide a dramatic alternative to colourful flowers and foliage on the winter scene. Here are three to chose from.
- Snake-bark maple (*Acer davidii*) has green bark striped with white, and reaches a height of 6m/18ft.
- Paperbark maple (*Acer griseum*) has papery, reddish bark that peels to a bright, red-brown under-bark. It grows to 7.5m/25ft.
- Scarlet willow (*Salix alba* 'Chermesina') has young stems that are orange-scarlet in winter. Restrict its height to 3m/9ft by cutting back hard in spring.

where you can appreciate it from your own fireside, instead of having to go out in the rain or snow to see it in its only flowering period. Even if you decide to have nothing else in your winter garden at least allow this cheerful plant to persuade you that all is not entirely gloomy until spring.

Another way to provide some interest during winter is to plant trees that have decorative bark. They will provide year round pleasure but many only really take centre stage when the leaves fall away and their bark is fully exposed. It is advisable not to choose a tree with a thick trunk for a small garden, but there are some delicate varieties that are suitable for this purpose.

Beautiful bark

An especially good choice would be the slim and graceful white-barked Himalayan birch (*Betula jacquemontii*). If you buy this tree when it is young and do not remove too many lower side branches, it will grow to about 2.7m/9ft in 10 years. The bark peels to a dazzling white and is shown to best effect if you plant it against a dark background

(but not too near the house, to avoid any structural damage by the roots).

A must for dramatic winter colour in any garden are the dogwoods. The Westonbirt dogwood, *Cornus alba* 'Sibirica' and *C. sanguinea* 'Winter Flame' can be grown for their bright red winter stems, vivid against snow or wonderful reflected in the surface of a pond.

The *Cornus alba* varieties also produce colourful foliage in autumn. They grow to a height of about 90cm/3ft, but must be pruned back almost to ground level in early spring to encourage plenty of new shoots for the next season.

Another possible addition to the garden in winter would be witch hazel (*Hamamelis mollis*). Defined either as a shrub or a small tree, the 'Pallida' variety produces pure yellow flowers with a wonderful perfume. Witch hazel does not like lime, however, so be sure you have a suitable, fairly acid soil before you buy because the plants are expensive. If your soil meets the requirements, try to get a four-year-old plant with nice, plump buds and no suckers, as younger plants can fail. If your soil is quite heavy

add a large amount of peat or garden compost to the site before planting. The plant will grow to about 1.8m/6ft, and branches brought indoors for flower arrangements will perfume the room beautifully. Take care when cutting, however, as witch hazel dislikes hard pruning.

If you have banks or slopes in your garden, nothing is

Soft freckled petals of the gently nodding hellebore (above) can soften the effect of a winter garden which often consists only of rugged looking plants like heathers. Their looks are deceptive as the Helleborus orientalis (Lenten rose) is an evergreen in mild areas.

Cyclamen × atkinsii (right) makes a spectacular sweep of vibrant purple shades when mass planted in a wide border.

PERFECT PARTNERS

Many people choose just one flowering specimen to add a bright splash of colour to their garden in the winter months but why choose just one? Once you have an idea of which plants provide winter interest select a few in colours which complement each other particularly well and plant them together. It doesn't matter whether your garden is small or palacial—you can achieve an oasis of cheerful shades. Vibrant crocuses in summery tones have been planted here amidst a clump of purple heathers (erica).

For something a little taller in the winter garden choose the Daphne mezereum (right). The bright blossoms of this bushy shrub appear in late winter/early spring. The dense clusters encase the leafless branches. They are replaced by light green leaves which are grey on their undersides. It gives pleasure all year round as well as making an active contribution to a winter colour scheme.

lovelier than seeing them carpeted in heather (erica). The foliage is evergreen and flowers come in many colours.

Heather carpet

There are over 500 species of flowering heather altogether, many of which bloom in winter so there is no lack of choice. Why not try a pink variety such as *E. × darleyensis*

WINTER FLOWERING SHRUBS

Any one of these shrubs will add shape, interest and colour to your garden all year round—but especially in winter. Make a feature of a single shrub, or plant a selection to create a winter shrub border.

PLANT	HEIGHT	FEATURES
Cornelian cherry (Cornus mas)	3m/9ft	This shrub has a rather open, spreading habit and produces a mass of tiny yellow flowers in late winter.
mezereon (Daphne mezereum)	90cm/3ft	This popular shrub has fragrant purple blooms in late winter, followed by scarlet berries.
oleaster (Elaeagnus macropylla)	3m/9ft	A pretty silvery evergreen, it produces fragrant flowers of a similar silvery colour in autumn.
false castor-oil plant (Fatsia japonica)	2.4m/8ft	An evergreen with thick stems and few branches, it has rather exotic white flowers in early winter. This plant does not like being pruned: just cut out any dead wood in spring.
mahonia (M. japonica)	2.4m/8ft	This shrub produces long lily-of-the-valley-scented clusters of yellow flowers in mid-winter. For the rest of the year, it provides evergreen background, but it can be invasive if not kept in check.
viburnum (V. farreri, syn. fragrans)	2m/6ft	Pale pink buds open to deliciously scented white flowers, that are frost-resistant. Young growth is bronze-coloured.
autumn cherry (Prunus subhirtella)	6m/18ft	This is, in fact, a tree, but is compact enough to be grown in a container. 'Autumnalis' has semi-double white blooms and can flower between late autumn and early spring; 'Autumnalis Rosea' has pale pink blooms. It is best grown in mild areas and prefers shelter.

'George Rendall' or the dazzling white 'Molten Silver'?

Heathers require little attention and spread freely, but they, too, dislike lime in the soil. An alternative solution would be to grow them in containers filled with ericaceous lime-free compost. 'George Rendall' and 'Molten Silver' (often sold as 'Silberschmelze') grow to around 45cm/18in tall, while the little *Erica carnea* 'Vivellii', with its carmine flowers and bronze foliage, reaching a height of only 20cm/8in, makes an ideal container plant. Ling (*Calluna vulgaris*) can be used in a similar way to heather, producing a marvellous show of foliage and flowers in reds, oranges, yellows and golds.

Christmas roses

For the front of the border, Christmas rose (*Helleborus niger*) is a good choice, with its nodding white flowers, tinged pink, that appear in the depths of winter. There is also the Lenten rose (*Helleborus orientalis*), that has red, pink, purple, cream or white blooms, and flowers for a long time. Both grow to only about 45cm/

18cm high, and are happy in dappled shade.

Amid all your planning, one garden essential you should not forget about are bulbs such as snowdrops, winter aconites and cyclamen. Snowdrops (galanthus) are best planted and moved 'in the green', which means that, unlike other bulbs, they are best divided after flowering but before the foliage dies back.

Winter bulbs

Winter aconites (*Eranthis hyemalis*) are cheerful but can be too invasive for a small garden. Tuberous *Cyclamen coum* are shy plants but a real delight. Mark them carefully when you plant them because you may forget where you put them. Suddenly, in early winter, one little variegated leaf will appear, a sign that you are about to get masses and masses of tiny, bright flowers right through to early spring.

If you want to bring colour to a balcony or if you only have a patio, there is still much you can do to cheer up the winter months. There are many undemanding little plants for tubs, sink gardens and window

Acers (above) are real all rounders in the garden. Renowned for their remarkably intense autumn colouring they make an excellent choice for a winter garden too. The paper-like outer bark of A. griseum unfurls to reveal the reddish bark beneath.

For a bright, sunny display of pansies (right) you have to plan well ahead. Plant them in early autumn or late summer while the ground is still warm and feed them with a proprietary fertilizer in early autumn to build up their strength for the long winter ahead. They will repay your hard work with a palette of colours.

COLOURFUL CATKINS

Before many of the spring flowers have appeared, certain trees produce catkins that can add their own sparkle of colour and interest to your garden. Why not try the non-weeping willow, *Salix aegyptiaca* or the Musk willow. Grey catkins that turn to bright yellow adorn its bare branches in late winter and early spring, and are followed by large, oval, dark green leaves. The tree reaches an eventual height of 5m/15ft.

With shiny yellow petals that resemble buttercups the pretty yellow flowers of the winter aconite, *Eranthis hyemalis*, (right) grace the garden in late winter. The long, thin, pale green leaves form a collar around the sunny flowerhead.

The winter flowering jasmine (left) is another yellow addition to the winter garden. The bright flowers are produced on leafless stems all through the winter months. This tough climber will survive in practically any position, even against a cold, shady wall. The flowers may be slightly susceptible to damage from very cold winds. Prune flowering stems after flowering to within a few centimetres of the base.

boxes (these would be suitable for rockeries, too). The charming small birch tree, *Betula* 'Golden Cloud', will grow happily in a container, but is rather delicate at first, so surround it with other pots in autumn to keep it sheltered from harsh winds. The plants will then keep each other protected on frosty nights, and a grouped display will look attractive when viewed from a window.

The winter flowering dwarf perennial Algerian iris, *Iris stylosa ungularis*, also sold as *I. unguicularis,* will, given enough sun, produce lavender blue flowers amid feathery foliage, and reach only about 30cm/1ft in height. It will flower again in summer so it earns its place in the border.

All year colour

Finally, there are Universal pansies and gem-coloured primroses. Use them to fill your winter garden with summer colour by planting them in borders, as edging flowers, in window boxes or in tubs – perhaps surrounding the base of a birch tree. For these, you will have to think well ahead. They are best planted early, while the ground is still warm, then fed well in early autumn to build them up. After this, you can leave them alone, apart from dead-heading the pansies as the blooms fade. You can probably buy them at the same time as your bulbs and, as they may well already be in flower, you will be able to choose from an almost infinite palette of colours.

With careful planning you can create a winter garden for little extra expense.

CHRISTMAS WREATHS

Take up the challenge of making your own wreaths. The hard part is already done because florists sell plastic filled with foam and shaped into a circle.

After soaking the shape push the stems of plant material into it. Try brightly-coloured fruits, small fir-cones, painted walnuts, ribbons or other cheerful decorations. For a traditional look use holly with mistletoe and ivy.

To these could be added 'Christmas fern' (*Polystichum acrostichoides*), which is shaped like holly, or variegated ivy. But however plain or elaborate you decide to make your wreath, make sure you put it in a prominent position like a gate, the front door or on an internal door.

This Christmas wreath (right) is made simply of hollies, berries and cones. A bright bow adds colour.

Autumn Leaves

The fiery tints of autumn leaves keep the garden ablaze with colour and interest long after the heady days of summer have gone.

The plant world undergoes a number of dramatic changes as the seasons unfold, but most of us would agree that there are none so spectacular as those which accompany the advance of summer into autumn. As deciduous trees and shrubs prepare for their brief winter rest, their decaying leaves flare up into a spectrum of glowing yellows, oranges and reds before cascading into vibrant pools that rustle underfoot.

The gorgeous effects are invaluable in the garden once the riot of summer bedding colour has begun to fade. Flowers traditionally provide the greatest interest but foliage, in all its variety of shape, size, texture and colour, plays an important part too. The light of autumn is often almost glowing in its warmth, showing the flush of leaf colour to advantage and doing much to dispel the gloom with which we view the shortening days and falling temperatures that mark the coming of winter.

The intensity of autumn leaf colour may vary from year to year, and the blaze is often brief, influenced by growing conditions and very much at the mercy of our unpredictable climate – a strong wind can strip a tree of its glory with frustrating speed! For such reasons, especially in small gardens where each plant must work hard to earn its space, the richest rewards will come from species chosen not just for their brilliant autumn dress but for what they offer at other times of year, such as fragrant spring flowers or bold summer foliage.

Trees provide most of the very best autumn colour. Of

Autumn leaves with paler, golden colours, such as the American tupelo, otherwise known as black gum (Nyssa sylvatica), are particularly beautiful when seen against the light of a setting sun (above), while the rich, dark red autumn foliage of plants in the Amelanchier genus is at its best glowing enticingly at the back of a border (right). Here, the tree is sited among evergreens and trees which turn later in the autumn, such as a silver birch; the cool green background throws the red leaves forward.

course, the taller species must be left to the open spaces of the countryside and parklands. Yet there are some, maturing to 6-7.5cm/20-25ft that can be easily accommodated in an average garden.

Even if it is just for the inspiration it provides, you should look out for the likes of the Persian ironwood (*Parrotia persica*) with its flaming autumn foliage of yellow, orange and red, and its attractive flaking bark. The tupelo (the American *Nyssa sylvatica* and the Chinese *N. sinensis*) burns with fiery brilliance in the autumn whilst the orange and red of *Amelanchier lamarckii* is matched in its splendour by a mass of starry white flowers in spring.

Smaller trees

A wealth of smaller trees and shrubs with colourful autumn livery give plenty of opportunities for the gardener more restricted by space. The witch hazels (*Hamamelis* spp.) are ideal as specimen trees, giving year-round interest with spidery, often fragrant flowers in winter and early spring, and handsome autumn foliage ranging from the lovely yellows of *H. mollis* through copper to red. The leaves of *H. vernalis* 'Sandra' are purple when young, turn mid-green in summer, and thence to a medley of reds, purples, copper and yellow.

Related to witch hazel is the shrub *Fothergilla major*, whose autumn radiance deserves a prime position in any garden. Its dark green summer foliage assumes a softly mottled complexion of yellow, gold and orange, flushed with red. If, at about 2.4m/8ft in height, this seems too big for your small garden, the similarly delightful witch alder (*F. gardenii*) offers a 1m/3ft alternative. Both also bring a profusion of fragrant, white brush-like flowers to the gar-

den's spring display.

Viburnums are most appreciated for their lovely, often fragrant, flowers, but some of the deciduous species have the additional attraction of good autumn colour. *Viburnum carlesii* and *V. grandiflorum* take on luscious wine-red to deep purple tints which can add darker, cooler contrast to more fiery neighbours.

In late summer, the smoke tree (*Cotinus coggygria*) produces a mass of tiny purple flower stalks. Though insignificant in themselves, they form distinctive plumes that fade to a smoky grey against blushing autumn leaves. 'Flame' is an excellent variety for orange-red brilliance, whilst the purple foliage of 'Notcutt's

The slow-growing shrub Fothergilla major has small, fragrant spring flowers, but is grown for its multi-coloured autumn display (above). The crimson glory vine (Vitis coignetiae) is well-named. Its leaves will smother a sunny wall in summer, then turn a deep wine red, verging on purple (below).

MARVELLOUS MAPLES

For many, the classic colours of autumn are most closely associated with the maples. Their graceful forms and lovely leaf shapes make them attractive the year round, but never more so than when the end of summer drives them into a blazing display of all imaginable shades of yellow through to scarlet and crimson. As well as the glorious leaf show, some varieties provide extra interest with ornamental bark.

A great number of maples are simply too large for the average garden, but the Japanese maples (*Acer palmatum* and *A. japonicum*) are the smallest and slowest-growing. They will remain a usable size for many years in most gardens and it is not surprising that they represent the most common ornamental maple, offering many different forms of leaf shape and colour.

Here is a short guide to some of the most attractive of the varieties: *Acer palmatum*
'Atropurpureum' – bronze-purple summer foliage which turns crimson.
'Dissectum' – forms a low, rounded bush with finely-cut leaves, turning red and occasionally yellow.
'Dissectum Atropurpureum' – bronze-purple, finely-cut leaves.
'Heptalobum Elegans' – deeply-toothed leaves turning crimson.
'Osakazuki' – deeply-toothed leaves turning various shades of orange, scarlet and crimson.
'Senkaki' – coral-red branches and yellow autumn foliage.
Acer japonicum 'Vitifolium' – large fan-shaped leaves turning red, orange and purple, often leaving the centre of the tree green.
'Aureum' – soft yellow foliage in summer, turning red.

The paper-bark maple (*Acer griseum*) is a taller tree, maturing to 7.5m/25ft or more, but is, again, very slow-growing. Its bark continually peels away to reveal cinnamon-coloured underbark. The foliage is orange, scarlet and crimson in autumn.

There are two particularly important points to bear in mind should you be thinking of one of these glorious trees for your garden. You will need to provide some shelter from the wind, and the soil should be neutral to acid, although most varieties will tolerate some lime.

Variety' gives additional summer interest, later turning an attractive, rich deep red.

Leaf forms

Leaf shape plays a large part in determining the strength of colour and the effect of the plant within your overall scheme. Large, simply-shaped leaves like those of the climbing crimson glory vine (*Vitis coignetiae*) create dramatic, sculptural backdrops for other plants throughout spring and summer, and emphasize the vibrant mix of coppers, reds and purples in the autumn.

More elaborate leaf forms, on the other hand, give a softer, prettier appearance. Of the popular and outstandingly beautiful Japanese maples (*Acer palmatum*), the variety 'Dissectum' has extraordinarily delicate leaves which bring a hazy look to the stunning autumn colour.

Easily recognized for its distinctive leaf shape is the stag's horn sumach (*Rhus typhina*) with sweeping branches of fern-like foliage, more delicately cut in the variety 'Laciniata', that turn a fiery concoction of red, orange and yellow.

Berries and leaves

Less common, but bright as a beacon in autumn, is the winged spindle (*Euonymus alatus*) and its smaller variety, 'Compactus'. The tapered leaves arch downwards in fantastic shades of crimson and scarlet, and fall away to reveal corky wings along the naked stems in winter.

Berries play a significant part in the end-of-year display, and in many cases the accompanying foliage colours as if in gaudy competition. In some species of sorbus, the jewel-like brilliance of massed autumn berries is matched by the flaming yellows, bronze and scarlet of its graceful pinnate leaves. Many of this genus are rather tall, but the tiny *S. reducta* grows to only a foot or two and turns bronze-red or purple with pink berries.

Cotoneaster, too, is best known for its fruit but, again, the foliage of some of the deciduous species competes for our attention with its blazing colour. The herring-bone pat-

The palmate leaves of Japanese maple (Acer palmatum) are attractive enough in the green, but in autumn take on gorgeous, clear red tones (top left).

Euonymus alatus 'Compactus' (above left) is a dense, low-growing shrub whose leaves turn purple, then bright scarlet, before they fall.

A relative of Virginia creeper, Parthenocissus tricuspidata 'Veitchii' is just as vigorous a climber. Red and gold at first (top right), its leaves later turn deep purple.

Berberis wilsoniae is a dwarf barberry whose turning leaves are set off by succulent berries (above right).

tumn colour, as most of us know from the scarlet, orange and crimson of the Virginia creeper (*P. quinquefolia*). But look also for *P. tricuspidata* 'Veitchii' which turns a gorgeous deep reddish-purple.

The white and pink variegations of the Chinese Virginia creeper (*P. henryana*) are a delight in summer and quite breath-taking when they assume the brilliant red tints of autumn. Of the vines, *Vitis* 'Brant' is particularly notable for its striking yellow and russet colouring traced with contrasting green veins.

Hedges

Hedging is too often thought of as evergreen, especially since many shrubs and trees will give an attractively changing screen to reflect the movement of the seasons. For gardeners with the space, beech (*Fagus*) is a splendid choice, easily trimmed for neatness, and colouring beautifully in autumn through to winter.

The barberry (*Berberis*) includes several deciduous species that assume flaming autumn tints, such as *B.* × *rubrostilla* and the dwarf *B. wilsoniae*, but *B. thunbergii* is great for hedging in the smaller garden, producing clusters of pale yellow spring flowers followed by small scarlet berries and rich red foliage. The variety 'Atropurpurea Nana' is an excellent dwarf form for edging borders or creating low dividing hedges, showing purple-red leaves through spring and summer.

A good mix of evergreen plants gives contrasting shades of greys, lush greens, even blues, to show the deciduous blaze the best effect, and these can offer attractive changes of colour too. Conifers often become bronzed or tinged with purple as autumn advances, and the glossy, dark green leaves of the Oregon grape (*Mahonia aquifolium*) assume purple tints towards the beginning of winter.

Perhaps because of the natural emphasis on foliage, many bamboos, grasses and ferns seem at their best in autumn, bringing further variations of shape and lighter, cooler colour. Some even bring their own autumn transformations. The grass *Hakonechloa macra* may produce feathery plumes of red-brown flowers, whilst the fronds of the Royal fern (*Osmunda Regalis*) mellow to a beautiful russet hue.

tern of *C. horizontalis* lends itself well to planting against walls, but the smaller *C. adpressus*, with wavy-edged leaves, is ideal for rock gardens and borders.

Keen cooks use the often edible fruits of vaccinium in desserts and preserves, but for radiant autumn colour alone the deciduous species are vaulable garden residents. Look for the bright red of *V. corymbosum* or the low-bush berry *V. angustifolium laevifolium*.

Climbers

Climbers are the great concealers of walls and unsightly features whilst providing excellent backdrops for further planting. The genus parthenocissus gives spectacular au-

PERFECT PARTNERS

Make the best of autumn leaf colour with clever companion planting. Because of their extraordinary brilliance, the winged spindle and Japanese maples are most impressive set against the cooler, contrasting colours of evergreens. But echo the season's blaze in fiery groups of red and yellow perennials such as *Helenium autumnale*, red-hot pokers and chrysanthemums. Accentuate the rich warmth of deep purple leaves with an underplanting of white and pink, using Michaelmas daisies or autumn crocuses and cyclamen.

The blue of Aster ericoides *cools the fires of* Rhus trichocarpa.

Landscaping

By applying a few simple principles used by landscape gardeners, you can turn a dull plot into something really special, full of interesting shapes and surprises.

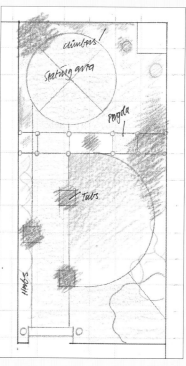

Few of us can afford the services of a professional landscape gardener. However, by applying the basic principles they use, and maybe putting in a bit of hard work at the start, you can make your garden infinitely more interesting, whatever its size. A typical town garden with a rectangle of grass surrounded by straight flowerbeds and raw-looking fences can be improved out of all recognition by redesigning its basic shape.

If you are starting a new garden, either from a bare patch left by the builders, or from an overgrown or neglected old plot, thinking on landscape gardening lines right from the start will stop you making mistakes that take time and money to put right later on. A well-designed garden will be easier to manage and can be perfectly attuned to your specific needs.

Design principles

The ground rules that professional landscape gardeners follow are basically simple, and can be learnt by studying

The first step in redesigning your garden is to make a scale plan of the site (below left), on which you can plot where the various elements – lawn, paths, beds, shed, paved seating area and so on – will go. Then, unless you envisage only small-scale changes or are skilled at D.I.Y., it is time to seek professional help in turning your plans into reality.

This may well mean you have to put up for a while with your garden resembling a cross between a building site and a war zone (above left) as the basic structure – the paths, paving and any wooden structures – is put in place. It is only when the plants come to be put in and the lawn laid that the site comes to resemble a garden, ready for you to add personal touches such as ornaments and garden furniture (far left).

Once a garden has been designed as well as this, maintaining it is simply a matter of looking after the plants and applying the odd coat of paint.

other gardens, either on the ground or in photographs. A visually pleasing garden always has plenty of curves – lawns and beds have gently undulating edges, and paths wind away into the distance.

Strategically placed focal points – a sundial, bird bath, large flower tub or specimen tree – draw your eye onwards and provide extra interest. If there is an interesting feature or pleasant view beyond the garden, this will be framed in foliage to accentuate it.

The garden will probably be designed so that you **cannot** quite see how far it extends, or exactly what happens when

Even a small yard garden can be landscaped (left); the same principles apply. Where a lawn was the feature of the similarly-shaped, slightly larger garden on the opposite page, here wooden decking has been used to provide slight changes of height, a pathway through the garden and a seating area. As the site is rather dark, foliage plants in containers and borders provide growing interest, while the narrowness of the garden has been made an advantage by laying wooden beams from wall to wall to create an arbour.

Dividing a garden up into small areas is a necessity for a long narrow plot. A wooden trellis (above) is perfect for this. It both screens and reveals, and acts as a windbreak and a support for climbers.

As an alternative, a smaller area can be divided up with paths; paving (below) creates strong geometric shapes, while other materials such as grass or gravel can make curved or serpentine edges.

you get to the end — it invites you to explore. This can be done quite simply by partially blocking the view with a trellis and an arch, or inserting a bed running crossways that is planted with tallish shrubs.

However lavishly planted, even wild, the garden may seem at first, it will always consist of clearly defined areas. Lawns, flowerbeds, paths and a paved sitting area are the most common features, but there may also be a vegetable garden, children's play area, a

pond — as many different areas of interest as the size of the plot can comfortably take.

Changes of level are also built into the design — terraces, steps and grassy banks in a large garden, raised beds or a rockery in a smaller one. Even if the garden is actually flat, the planting will provide eye interest at different levels — ground cover, herbaceous plants, taller shrubs, climbing plants and trees.

Changes of texture are equally important — a close-

clipped lawn sets off a luxuriant herbaceous border; hard paving contrasts with soft delicate flowers; smooth, still water reflects rugged stone.

Providing privacy is an important part of the landscape gardener's brief. Boundaries will be designed to provide this unobtrusively, without creating a prison-yard feeling.

The first step in redesigning your garden is to decide to what use you are going to put

A well-planned garden has something for everyone. A sandpit (above) encourages young children to use the garden and provides the garden with a focal point. It can be converted into a formal pond later.

Remarkable effects can be obtained by reversing the usual order of things (below). Here a raised central lawn is encircled by a water feature, with more conventional beds filling in around the edges.

it. Is it to be an outdoor room, used mainly for relaxation? Or do you have time to care for lots of flowers and a lawn? Will it need to cater for children playing? What about special features like a pond, rockery, sunken garden, barbecue, or easy-to-maintain raised beds?

Shapes and sizes

The next step is to measure your plot on all sides, to see if it is actually rectangular, or whether it tapers or is irregularly shaped. Make a note of any slopes, and find out which parts of the garden are in sun or shade at which times of day. List features you wish to keep, like established trees or shrubs, and those you want to get rid of, like piles of rubble or dilapidated sheds.

Draw a scale plan of the garden on squared paper. Include the position of the house and anything you are quite certain is going to stay, like a large tree or paved area.

Get several photocopies made, and use one to draw a plan of the garden as it is. Use the others to see how you can create the garden of your dreams. Rough out the broad concept first – in pencil to allow for changes of mind – leaving details of planting and so

on until later.

Do not try to cram too many features into a small garden. Drawing your ideas to scale on paper will make you realize what you can and cannot get into your particular plot.

Paths need to be at least 60cm/2ft wide for easy movement. However, paths are not essential; unless the ground is very boggy, close-mown grass can take their place.

A large lawn that fills most of the width makes a small garden look bigger – like fitted carpet in a small room. The depth of the flower beds should ideally be in proportion to the size of the plot.

Long and narrow

Make the most of a typical long narrow plot by including features that run across the garden – beds with tall planting, internal hedges or trellis work – at intervals on alternate sides. Another way of creating the illusion of width is to set the lawn at an angle of 45° to the house.

A small, square garden looks best with interest in the centre – a round lawn or a central pool or tree. Take away the squareness with curved beds in the corners. An irregular shape lends itself to the

Ugly but functional buildings need covering up (above). This unsightly garage has all but vanished under a Boston ivy (Parthenocissus tricuspidata).

By introducing steps into your garden, you create changes of height and divide up the garden (below). They are also a handy place to put container plants.

BRIGHT IDEAS

DISGUISES

Some unsightly features can be disguised or totally transformed by planting.

- Dead tree. Grow honeysuckle or a clematis up it and put a circular seat round the base, or cut the top level and turn it into a bird table.
- Cracked concrete. Plant creeping plants like thyme in the crevices. Enlarge broken areas, fill with compost and plant alpines.
- Ugly outbuilding. Clad concrete walls with weatherboard. Fix horizontal wires to timber and plant an evergreen honeysuckle. Russian vine or *Clematis montana* will soon cover both walls and roof.
- Straight concrete path. Soften edges with tumbling, low-growing plants.

creation of several distinct 'mini-gardens', divided by internal hedges or screens.

Some gardens taper off very unsatisfactorily into a triangle at the bottom. Depending on its size, you can cut this off with a big, ground-hugging evergreen shrub, or screen it off with trellis and climbing plants. Create a secret garden in the enclosure – or use it as an area in which to tuck away the shed or compost heap.

Treat a minute garden or walled yard like an outdoor room, with attractive paving, lots of pretty plant containers, raised beds and garden ornaments. Train climbers up the walls for vertical interest. High walls often mean deep shade – paint them white to a height of 1.8m/6ft (so frequent repainting is easy) for maximum light reflection, and choose light-coloured paving. A sunny walled yard, warm and sheltered, is an ideal site for a scented garden.

Once you have roughed things out on paper, get outside and see how it will look in three dimensions. Use bamboo

canes to mark the position of any tall features or partitions; pegs and string to map out possible new paths; and a hosepipe or rope to experiment with curves in a flower bed or lawn.

Making it work

Check that the features you planned on paper will work. Herbaceous borders need a sunny spot to flower really well. A pond should get a reasonable amount of sun and be

DESIGN FOR SAFETY

Make sure all changes of level are clear to see, and paths smooth. Repair or replace steps with crumbling edges.

If there are toddlers in the family ensure all boundaries and gates, especially in front, are secure. Do not have a pond.

Cut back tree branches overhanging circulation routes.

Provide lighting for paths used after dark.

SAFETY FIRST

away from trees. Although a patio is usually sited close to the house, if it is on the shady side of the building think about putting it elsewhere.

A lawn needs sun for at least part of the day to flourish – but you can buy special seed mixes for shade. Use the least sunny parts of your garden for shade-loving shrubs, ground cover plants, and utilitarian items like sheds and compost bins, screened if necessary.

Slight slopes are manageable, but on sharp ones soil gets washed to the bottom, and grass is difficult to mow. Some form of terracing is the answer to this problem.

Sometimes the problem can be solved by dividing the slope into two or more terraces by inserting shallow log steps, and confining the soil with peat blocks, old railway sleepers or low drystone walls. On sharper slopes the downward pressure is much greater and solidly built masonry walls and steps will be needed – this is almost certainly a job for a professional.

Another way of dealing with

Paths that wind off out of sight always add to the sense of space in a garden, and give it an air of intrigue and mystery (above left), though this is not always easy to appreciate when seen from above. It is always a good idea to try and visualize how a new garden scheme will look from the ground as well as from the house.

Although bricks and paving are the usually favoured material for making steps and paths, there are other possibilities (above right). Railway sleepers are strong and weather resistant and will take a dark wood preservative, enabling you to make a flight of steps with contrasting gravel 'treads' and wooden 'risers'.

a slope is to turn it into a rock garden by building rocks into it. However, this is heavy work and may prove expensive; stone is costly, and what looks like a lot does not go very far once half-buried in the ground.

Getting help

Nasties like crumbling concrete or tarmac hardstanding, disused sheds and ancient rubbish tips cannot be designed round or lived with – they must be swept away. Hire a skip if you can manage the clearance yourself, or look in the Yellow Pages under garden services and get some idea of cost.

Garden labourers are also invaluable if you have a totally overgrown plot needing rotovating, an old hedge or dead tree trunk to be grubbed out, earth to be moved or a pond dug. Alternatively you can hire rotovators, hedge-cutters, heavy-duty mowers and flame guns by the day or weekend.

If you have a big tree that needs thinning, look in the Yellow Pages under tree work – never tackle it yourself.

Light and Shade

Deep shade and harsh, unremitting sunlight can both cause problems in the garden; the solution lies in altering the conditions or finding the plants to suit them.

Many plants are at their best in sunny situations, while others prefer partial or dappled shade. Extremes of sunlight and of shade can create problems for plants and for gardeners alike.

A town garden that faces north and is surrounded by buildings and garden walls may occasionally be a welcome cool haven. Most of the time, though, it feels and is sunless and dull. In a larger, more open garden, there may still be dark and shady sites that you wish to lighten up.

Fortunately there are many practical ways to brighten and lighten a shady garden or to create shade and shelter in an exposed and sunny site.

Let there be light

If shade is caused by mature trees, the remedy is to thin out the crown. This is difficult and dangerous work and should only be carried out by qualified and properly insured professional tree surgeons.

If the trees are young and the branches accessible it is possible to raise or 'lift' the head of a tree by removing some of the lower branches.

You are entitled to cut back any tree branches overhanging your boundary fence or wall, though, in the interest of neighbourliness, it is best to tell your neighbour politely

Light and shade is an important element in gardening; it determines which plants will grow well in a particular site and which areas of the garden will be most suitable for sitting areas, ponds, or other features, as well as being a design element in its own right. Dappled shade (above) makes agreeable, everchanging patterns as the sun moves through the sky.

You can make the most of the available light in deeply shaded areas by painting walls white, or another light, reflective shade, and by using white furnishings (above).

The simplest solution to excessively bright or shady areas of the garden is to find plants to suit the environment. A sunny spot will accommodate a riotous display of colourful bulbs and annuals (right), while plants which grow naturally in woodland or woodland edge conditions, such as the foxgloves (below) suit shade. This delightful yellow species is Digitalis ambigua.

what you intend doing.

If the tree is in your garden, and you decide that removing it entirely is the only solution, you will definitely need expert help. It will also be necessary to discover from your local council if a preservation order applies to your tree.

Hedge shade

If hedge shrubs or trees, especially the fast-growing Leyland cypress, are left to grow tall, this defeats the object of the hedge, as there is a loss of lower dense foliage cover. The best solution is to cut back the hedge's top growth, though not too drastically. It may take several years to reduce a rampant hedge to the required height without damaging its top.

Shade caused by buildings and garden walls can be mitigated by painting the walls, creating more reflected light. White is the popular choice, but if you prefer a colour, keep to pale or pastel shades.

With higher light levels you will be able to grow a wider variety of plants, especially variegated foliage plants that need extra light to look their best. The reflected light will also make the garden a brighter and pleasanter place for you to relax in.

If the shady area is small and close to the house, you might consider lighting it. Then, when you sit outside on summer evenings it will be bright enough to enjoy. Keep unwanted insect guests at bay with insect-repelling amber or yellow light bulbs.

Mirror images

In a small town garden, mirrors fixed to courtyard and boundary walls give an illusion of space as well as reflecting available light.

Used without embellishment, a mirror makes a fairly bald statement, but it can be made to look natural by framing it with climbing plants. A ledge or shelf in front of the mirror makes a useful site for pots or containers with trailing or hanging plants.

Prepare the mirror for outdoor use by lining its back with aluminium foil. Mount and frame the back and edges of the mirror with treated wood and use mirror glass thicker than 5mm/^{1}/$_5$ in.

In a shady garden area, use white metal or plastic outdoor furniture to add to the light effects. White Versailles tubs in wood or plastic will reflect available light and add to the overall brighter look.

Use light or white coloured statuary or ornaments to make dramatic focal points in

GROWING TIPS

WATER IN TIME

Plants in dry shade under trees, hedges or in a rain shadow area at the base of a wall will need extra water in very hot conditions.

Keep a watering can on hand so that you can provide them with a weekly watering before they become parched.

shady areas. The deep shade of a laurel glade, for instance, can be lifted by the addition of accents such as a white bench or a striking piece of mock-classical statuary.

If the shaded area has an ordinary, well-drained, loam soil, there are many flowering and foliage plants you can grow to lift the gloom. Many aquilegias do well in shade, including *A. alpina* 'Hensol Harebell', which bears deep blue flowers in early summer.

Foxgloves enjoy woodland shade conditions, and will seed themselves abundantly for future flowers. A short form, growing to 90cm/3ft, *Digitalis ambigua* is a bold and bright choice with golden-yellow trumpets. In spring, the sunny flowers of a variety of spring daisy, *Doronicum plantagineum* 'Harpur Crewe', will bring shafts of golden light to shine in the shade.

White-flowered plants are very stylish and offer the simplest way to brighten up the

area. *Phlox paniculata* 'Alba' and *Campanula latifolia* 'Alba' provide tall heads of white flowers in late or mid summer.

Variegated ivy will do well in dappled shade and will clamber up vertical surfaces towards the light. The glossy leaves of the variegated *Pachysandra terminalis* 'Variegata' offer good ground cover.

Covering up

If your garden is exposed to too much sunlight, there are several practical remedies. For quick results, building wooden trellis and screen block walling is the best choice.

For permanent overhead shading, install a pergola clad with attractive climbing plants. For a not-so-permanent effect, a large rectangular umbrella will provide a stylish, holiday atmosphere on a sun-drenched patio. In winter store it indoors or in a garden shed. Then you will have maximum winter light and a shaded area in summer.

Screening trellis work, open

Plants with strong, sculptural shapes such as New Zealand flax (Phormium tenax) can make good use of open, sunny sites, where they will cast strong shadows. The variety 'Purpureum' (above left) adds to its appeal with good leaf colour.

An alternative way of providing interest in a dark corner is with a piece of statuary or other stone feature (left).

The dry shade of a large tree makes planting difficult, but the addition of a bench or other seating makes a cool haven from which to enjoy the sunnier parts of the garden (above).

Shady woodland conditions suit Campanula latifolia, whose delicate white bells shine softly through the late summer (right).

Sites near to the house are often either too dark or too bright. Those on the shady side are best planted with a display of foliage plants (left), while sunnier situations suit colourful annuals and herbs, protected from the drying sun by a seasonal screen created by growing a deciduous climber on an open trellis (right).

Wood spurge (Euphorbia amygdaloides) is a shade-loving plant with sunny flowers made up of yellow bracts. 'Rubra', also known as 'Purpurea' (below) adds reddish-purple stems to its considerable charms.

A north-facing wall at the end of a narrow garden presents planting problems. One solution is to plant fragrant climbers to find the light and to create a kind of minimal arbour with a seat that looks back along the garden (below right). If the seating is painted white, as here, so much the better.

block walls and pergolas can all be used to support plants, which will soften the look of their supports. Although you are aiming to create shade, use plants that provide delicate screening or are deciduous, so that you have high light levels in winter. Climbing roses, wisteria and many varieties of clematis offer good seasonal shading.

Shadow play

Trees such as birch are suitable as seasonal screens. In summer, their delicate leaves and thin branches make a dappled shade. In winter, when the leaves have fallen, the framework of branches and twigs makes an interesting tracery effect against the sky, and allows all the available light to filter through.

On a patio or in a garden where there is strong and in-

A TRICK OF THE LIGHT

If you have a long narrow garden you can make two types of garden by some creative deception. Near the house plant trees and shrubs closely so that it appears that you have a small garden. All that will be visible from the house is a densely planted, shady area.

Make the rest of the garden open and lighter-looking; keep the plantings in this part of the garden near the edges and going up walls.

Using this device you will have the chance to use both plants that thrive in shade and those that prefer a more open aspect to create two separate gardens with very different atmospheres.

BRIGHT IDEAS

tense sunlight, use plants to make large and emphatic shadows. A large terracotta tub planted with an striking, architectural plant such as New Zealand flax (*Phormium tenax*), will make a strong statement. Place it so that its huge shadow can be cast onto a white wall or spread dramatically across a close-cut lawn.

An unadorned pergola will look effective if its strong parallel lines can be picked up as shadows on a wall. You can also cheat a little bit by painting darker areas onto a wall and pretending they are the shadows of the overhead pergola. It will create a talking point, and may make you feel the area is more shaded than it actually is.

At night, carefully planned lighting concealed behind dramatic plants will make interesting and effective shadow play. If your patio is used at night as an extended dining area, the lighting will provide you with a sense of extra space and add a theatrical effect to outdoor entertaining.

Delicate Touches

Feathery plumes or soft clouds of abundant tiny flowers mingle with delicate, airy blooms to bring ethereal notes to the garden.

Among the spectacular providers of glorious floral colour and eye-catching, dramatic foliage, there are other plants whose nature is less extrovert and showy, but whose contribution to the garden is no less important.

In mixed plantings, plants with a fragile, airy look serve to soften and lighten, providing welcome pauses for the eye between bolder, heavier shapes and strong colours. The smaller species are especially useful wherever an arbour or seat requires a more restful or romantic setting, and many will contribute airy, delicate touches to indoor flower arrangements throughout the year.

Smoky clouds

Most of these invaluable plants produce their ethereal effects through a profusion of tiny flowers which, though insignificant in themselves, form graceful, feathery plumes or shimmering, misty clouds. One of the most familiar examples is the appropriately-named smoke bush (*Cotinus coggygria*). This deciduous, bushy shrub grows to 5m/16ft or more. From July, masses of tiny purple flowers are carried in feathery panicles which fade with the summer to pro-

The smoke bush (Cotinus coggygria) is best grown on its own (left), while Crambe cordifolia is also good at the back of a border (above). Here, it sets off a pink geranium and a purple knapweed. The buff pink plume poppy (Macleaya microcarpa 'Coral Plume') also gives background height (right), but the tiny Gypsophila paniculata 'Flamingo' (below) is best in the centre of a bed.

duce a breathtaking, smoky haze against the brilliant autumn colouring of its leaves. While the purple-leaved varieties are quite splendid, the standard green-leaved form is the best in flower, whether it is part of a border or set on its own in a lawn.

If you have the space, the giant sea-kale (*Crambe cordifolia*) makes a magnificent feature in summer. From clumps of large, deep-green, wavy-edged leaves, this hardy perennial casts up intricately-branched stems bearing clouds of tiny white flowers to some 1.8m/6ft in height. It really needs companions of a similar size if it is not to overpower a border. Since most of us do not have the space for huge herbaceous combinations, try it as a specimen plant, but be sure to place it where it is sheltered from strong winds.

The plume poppy (*Macleaya* spp.) is another massive perennial, excellent for the back of a large border but again, for most of us better used on its own. Above splendid clumps of large, deeply-lobed leaves, it bears tall, feathery plumes, up to 1m/3ft long, of tiny flowers; creamy white in *M. cordata*

and buff-pink in *M. microcarpa* 'Coral Plume'. It dislikes disturbance but, once settled in a sunny position in well-drained soil, it can grow as high as 2.4m/8ft. Be warned that it can be very invasive.

Baby's breath

On a much smaller scale, and ideal for creating softer pockets within sunny mixed borders, is gyposphila, a genus of annuals and herbaceous perennials much-loved by gardeners and flower arrangers alike. All carry masses of the tinest flowers whose effects are enhanced by the insubstantial branching stems of long, thin grey-green leaves. *G. elegans* is an easy annual, fast-growing to 60cm/24in, of erect and bushy habit, and it is wonderfully long-flowering. Throughout the summer, it is clothed in clouds of tiny white or pink flowers that give it its common name, baby's breath.

The slightly taller perennial *G. paniculata* has a shorter flowering period, from June to August, but it is unrivalled for its soft, vaporous effect. More of a spreader in habit, its tiny double flowers range in colour from the pristine white of

'Bristol Fairy' to the soft pink of 'Flamingo' and 'Rosy Veil'.

Another excellent perennial for decorative arrangements in the house is sea lavender or statice (*Limonium latifolium*), which makes an effervescent edging plant. From mid to late summer, the rosettes of deep-green leaves are overcast by frothy clouds of lavender-blue flowers, especially useful to soften the edges of raised beds.

Good varieties include the light lavender-blue 'Blue Cloud' and the violet 'Violetta'. The flowers can be dried for everlasting arrangements if they are picked just before they open, but they are just as useful in winter decorations if left to brown on the plant.

Bugbane and rue

Gardeners with a lightly-shaded border and moist soil would do well to find a place for the bugbane (*Cimicifuga* spp.). Its tall, bottle-brush wands of small cream or white flowers are quite heavenly in summer, towering above

GRASSES

Grasses in flower can provide wonderfully graceful effects as border or specimen plants.
- Foxtail barley or squirreltail grass (*Hordeum jubatum*), growing to 60cm/2ft, is virtually unrivalled for the gossamer-like softness of its bowing flower spikes in summer and early autumn.
- At the same time, the arching spikelets of pennisetum carry lovely bottle-brush-like flower heads. Feather-top (*P. villosum*) also reaches about 60cm/2ft, carrying 10cm/4in long, softly bearded, cream or purple bristles, while fountain grass (*P. setaceum*), at 1m/3ft tall, bears narrow heads of silky tufts. Though perennial, these grasses are hardy only in the mildest areas and generally need to be overwintered in a cool greenhouse.
- Feather grass (*Stipa* spp.) is more hardy, and its elegant feathery plumes make handsome summer focal points in lawns. The large, diffuse plumes of *S. calamagrostis* (syn. *Achnatherum calamagrostis*) may reach 1.2m/4ft and their silvery-buff colouring shimmers sublimely in the breeze.
- *Hakonechloa macra* 'Aureola' does not always come into flower, but, when it does, the loose panicles of reddish-brown spikes create a breathtaking feathery effect in early autumn, when the leaves turn a similar colour. It forms a graceful dome of about 40cm/16in in height, and looks lovely spilling over the edges of lawns and paths.

Statice (Limonium latifolium) *is generally grown for drying, but its splendid lavender-blue flowers (far left) also make a fresh, effervescent show in the garden.*

The nodding racemes of Cimicifuga simplex, *carried high above the foliage, range from pure white to the pink and creamy tinges of varieties such as 'Elstead' (far left below).*

*The perennial meadow rue (*Thalictrum dipterocarpum *syn. T. delavayi) forms clumps of divided foliage topped with panicles of nodding, pink to lilac flowers, double in 'Hewitt's Double' (left).*

*The creamy heads of white mugwort (*Artemisia lactiflora*) provide an exuberantly frothy display in summer (below left), when they make an excellent foil to other, more strongly-coloured plants.*

handsome, divided foliage. The 1.5m/5ft spires of most species tend to be majestically erect, but the white racemes of *C. simplex* are carried on gracefully arching purple stems, and seem to float above the foliage from late summer into autumn. 'Elstead' is a reliable variety, but the purest white is 'White Pearl'.

Similar conditions suit meadow rue (*Thalictrum dipterocarpum*), which carries abundant, loose sprays of tiny mauve flowers with prominent yellow anthers through summer. White mugwort (*Artemisia lactiflora*) is also happy here, bearing diffuse, creamy, pyramidal plumes that make an excellent foil to stronger-coloured neighbours.

Taking a step down in size, the colourful plumes of the astilbes can be a little too stiff to be delicate, but try the 1m/3ft tall *Astilbe* 'Venus' and *A.* 'Ostrich Plume', which are both a

SUPPORTS

When plants such as the plume poppy and meadow rue are expected to achieve great heights, don't forget to provide some support (essential in exposed situations) to keep them at their best. Make sure canes are of a good length, but not tall enough to show above the foliage. White mugwort (*Artemisia lactiflora*) is one of the few tall, feathery plants which is self-supporting.

GARDEN NOTES

feathery soft pink, the latter gently arching above lovely, deeply-divided foliage.

Purple leaves

Heuchera 'Palace Purple' makes a striking edging for lightly-shaded borders. Its clump-forming, heart-shaped leaves are a deep purple, providing interesting ground cover and a fine background for the summer show of cloudy sprays, 45cm/18in high, of small white flowers.

In deeper, cooler shade and moist soil, the 20cm/8in tall woodland foamflower (*Tiarella cordifolia*) lives up to its name. Its dense carpet of dark-veined evergreen leaves make it excellent ground cover, and from spring to midsummer it casts up many soft spikes of star-like white flowers.

Delicate blooms

All these plants are effective when their myriad of tiny flowers are seen from a distance, but there are others whose blooms are given an ethereal quality by such features as long stamens, narrow petals or feathery bracts. These will bring more colour to borders and provide excellent material for smaller plantings around arbours, seats or doorways, where you come close enough to enjoy the fragile beauty of the individual flowers themselves.

Aquilegia longissima is an elegant perennial growing to about 60cm/24in, with fern-like foliage and lovely pale yellow flowers with long, dainty spurs. It likes sun and well-drained soil, as does *Eryngium alpinum*. Of a similar height, this has purple-blue teasel-like heads with a prominent collar of feathery bracts.

Annuals are always good for bridging gaps in flowering seasons and for adding lots of colour fairly quickly. The many-petalled flowers of love-in-a-mist (*Nigella damascena*) bring delicate touches to borders and cut flower arrangements throughout the summer. Encircled by a ruff of thread-like bracts, the flowers are borne 60cm/24in high on slender, erect stems with

The lovely texture of the pink and white astilbes is an asset in a mixed border (above). Here it is paired with the giant cowslip (Primula florindae).

The bold, highly-coloured leaves of Heuchera 'Palace Purple' provide a marked contrast to the delicacy of its flowers (below).

finely-cut foliage. The blue 'Miss Jekyll' and the mixed blue, purple, pink and white 'Persian Jewels' are magnificent semi-double varieties.

The spider flower (*Cleome spinosa* syn. *C. hassleriana*) takes its common name from the long stamens which protrude from its narrow-petalled flowers, which are borne in large rounded heads from mid summer into autumn. It's a bushy plant, quickly reaching about 1.2m/4ft, and its hairy stems with divided leaves enhance the spidery effect. The scented flowers are generally white flushed with pink, but 'Helen Campbell' is pure white, and 'Colour Fountain' gives a mix of shades from white to purple.

Light bulbs

Bulbs bring further light, airy touches to spring and autumn. The long-lasting spring display of the feather grape hyacinth (*Muscari comosum* 'Plumosum' or 'Monstrosum') is a splendid smoky haze of purple-blue filaments.

For autumn, plant *Nerine bowdenii*, the toughest of this mainly half-hardy genus. Its erect stems, up to 60cm/24in tall, carry loose umbels of pink flowers with long stamens and narrow strap-shaped petals that widen and curve back at their wavy-edged tips.

The ornamental onion genus, Allium, *is full of plants with remarkable spherical umbels that dry to lovely, fragile seed heads.* A. christophii, *also known as* A. albopilosum *(right) is one of the best, with 50 or so star-shaped flowers in every head.*

Many clematis have decorative seed heads – a characteristic which earned the wild species its common name of old man's beard – but few more so than the fluffy, silver tassels of the late-flowering C. tangutica *(below).*

SEED HEADS

Fading flowers often leave behind seed pods, which continue to bring fascinating shapes and textures to the garden and to decorative arrangements indoors.

Clematis often produces loose pompons of silky hairs which on *C. tangutica* mingle softly with the small, bright yellow lantern flowers in late summer and early autumn. Then, too, the massed seed heads of the clump-forming, herbaceous *C. recta* create a nebulous cloud in borders.

The heads of clematis and the feathery silver balls of the spring-flowering pulsatillas may be dried upside-down for fuzzy additions to dried indoor decorations. Do the same with the ornamental onion (*Allium* spp.) particularly the almost wispy heads of *A. aflatunense* and the magnificent skeletal globes with shiny black seeds of *A. christophii*. Hang these individually so as not to crush the fragile umbels.

The seed pods of love-in-a-mist (*Nigella damascena*) ripen into pale, spiky globes – green at first, then brown – which earn the plant its other common name of devil-in-a-bush. The heads dry well upside-down amid a haze of thread-like bracts and fragments of foliage.

The Cottage Garden Look

Bring a touch of the countryside to your garden with an informal bank of cottage-style blooms, and have a flower-filled display all summer.

You don't have to live in a thatched cottage to copy the 'look' of a cottage garden, with its overflowing beds of pretty, perfumed flowers. The cottage garden look is something you can achieve wherever you live and whatever the size of your garden.

You may not want to change the look of your whole garden, but you could choose a few cottage-garden plants that appeal to you and devote a small area of your garden to them, or simply add them to your existing flower beds. As well as looking pretty, a mixture of scented species near the house can fill the air with a wonderful heady fragrance on summer evenings. In a real pocket handkerchief sized plot, you can create a very authentic cottage garden look just by filling every scrap of space with flowers and you will find that this weed-smothering style is easy to maintain.

What is a cottage garden?
Centuries ago, a typical cottage garden would have been very different to our image of it today. A 'real' cottage garden would have been more like a smallholding; with vegetables, herbs, fruit trees and livestock – hens, ducks and geese, rabbits and a pig or perhaps even a cow. Flowers – if there were any – would have been limited mainly to wild plants that found their way in from the surrounding countryside. Basically, the true cottage garden would have looked a bit of a mess!

By Victorian times the 'cottage garden' had become very fashionable, and the typical example bore little relation to its original predecessor.

Today's cottage garden is likely to be a charming and rather disorderly blend of flowers and herbs spilling over brick or gravel paths and daisy-studded grass, with plants arranged to give a wild, natural look as though the garden just 'happened'.

Old-fashioned roses
A cottage garden relies on a mixture of flowers, including roses, for its effect. While modern varieties of rose can look perfectly in keeping in a cottage garden, if you really want to be authentic it pays to choose the sort that are nowadays called old-fashioned. A modern hybrid tea rose, for example, would never look right, but an old-fashioned, rambling

Select old-fashioned favourites (roses).

Let plants spread, providing ground cover.

Plant with a wall, fence or hedge as background.

Stately giants, like delphiniums, need staking.

Plant close together, in small groups.

Tall plants don't have to be set at the back

FOR YOUR OWN GARDEN

This rather grand cottage garden can easily be scaled down to fit a smaller patch; the basic structure of a cottage garden is the same whether for a stately home or your back garden. Using the ideas given here you can copy the style to transform as much or as little of your garden as you wish.

Use patches of white to offset strong colours.

Choose perennials or plants that self-seed (sweet William).

Include dainty flowers (aquilegia) as well as the bolder types.

Some plants can be left to sprawl happily (catmint).

A mixture (right) of sweet William, campion, crane's bill, daisy-like chrysanthemums, pansies and cornflowers provides a profusion of small-petalled blooms.

Having such a packed flower bed not only fills the garden with colour, but has the added advantage of suppressing weed growth.

As beautiful indoors as out – a selection (below) of sweet peas, pansies, miniature roses and cosmos in shades of pastel pink, white and burgundy, informally arranged in a jug.

finished blooming.

If it is important to you to have plants with a long flowering season, then choose bourbon or hybrid perpetual roses. These varieties can be relied on to produce flowers, albeit gradually fewer, during the later summer months and into autumn after the main flush of flower is over.

Essential plants

Although a mixture of different plants is an important factor of the cottage garden look, some plants are a 'must' and almost guarantee the romantic effect you are trying to achieve. Delphiniums, poppies, foxgloves, wallflowers, columbine and pot marigolds are prime examples.

Another 'classic' component of the cottage garden is a climber. This will give an appropriate look of unruliness and fullness to your cottage garden bed or border. Pretty examples are winter jasmine, climbing roses or honeysuckle. Train any one of these on to a wall, fence or trellis, or around the front door or porch. Clematis, too, has a suitably random appearance, and grows at an astonishing and satisfying rate. You may prefer to train one of these climbers over an arch made from wood or wire for a truly rustic effect.

Fruit and vegetables

Fruit trees – especially apples – always had a place in a real cottage garden. Nowadays

rose with delicate, flat-faced, pale-toned flowers would be ideal. Old-fashioned roses have the added advantage of usually being quite strongly perfumed.

Old-fashioned roses are easy to grow. They rarely need pruning, and suffer much less from disease than modern varieties. They have a shorter flowering period than hybrid teas however: sometimes only four to six weeks in the middle of summer. This is why they are usually grown amongst other old-fashioned flowers, chosen specially to carry on flowering when the roses have

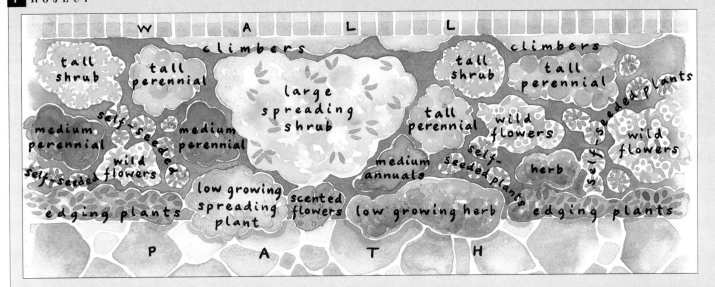

The plan (above) is an example of how you could plant up a flower bed for a cottage garden look. A list of suitable plants is given, left. The ideal depth for this flower bed is 1.2-1.5m/4-5ft.

Climbers – clematis, climbing rose, fan-trained fig, apricot, peach or apple tree
Edging plants – dwarf box, lavender, thyme, London pride
Large spreading shrubs – lavatera (mallow), *Viburnum fragrans,* lilac, azaleas, hydrangea
Low-growing herbs – thyme, marjoram
Low-growing spreading plants – *Stachys lanata* 'Silver Carpet' (lamb's ears)
Medium annuals – busy Lizzie (impatiens), petunia, salvia
Medium perennials – *Alchemilla mollis* (lady's mantle), ornamental grass, astrantia (masterwort)
Scented flowers – night scented stock, tobacco plant (nicotiana), dianthus (pinks)
Self-seeders – forget-me-not, poppies, aquilegia, foxgloves, honesty, nasturtiums, marigolds
Tall perennials – echinops (globe thistle), delphinium, lily, lupin, foxgloves, hollyhock
Tall shrubs – *Ribes sanguineum* (flowering currant), *Hamamelis mollis* (Chinese witch hazel)
Wild flowers – cornflowers, geranium (crane's-bill), foxglove

gardeners tend to plant them not only for fruit, but for the spring blossom and as supports for climbers which scramble up through their branches. Again, really old varieties with evocative names like 'Devonshire Quarrenden', 'D'Arcy Spice' and 'Cornish Aromatic' are still occasionally available from specialist growers. Though not heavy croppers, the flavour of these apples is truly delicious – far better than most fruit you buy from the supermarket.

Vegetables – the mainstay of real old cottage gardens – don't have to make the place look like an allotment. They can be grown in your border, mixed in with the flowers, where they look most attractive. When vegetables are grown to eat, it is the fruit of the plant that is all-important, but they often have interesting foliage and flowers too.

Try scarlet runner beans or climbing pea varieties growing on a wigwam of rustic bean-poles at the back of a flower bed; globe artichokes along-side delphiniums; or an edging of parsley or thyme by a path.

Romantic disorder
The essence of the traditional, romantic cottage garden is its overcrowded look, with plants filling every bit of space and spilling out over paths and grass. In the past, this look took many years to achieve – largely as a result of neglect! Nowadays we tend to create a more orderly version of the same look, with the emphasis on carefully selected cottage garden plants. Invasive plants still have their place – they are best grown together in a bed of their own where they make an ideal low-maintenance cottage border. The most important beds, however, or those where growing conditions are best, should be reserved for the less pushy plants which can then grow quite safely without risk

PERFECT PARTNERS

A vibrant and daring mixture of reds (lupins and sweet William), pink (peonies) and purple (campanula) creates an unusually striking effect.

of suffocation. If choice plants happen to self-seed, then you can think yourself lucky and either leave them where they fall or transplant them to another part of the garden.

Attractive combinations

Having decided which kinds of plants you want to grow, the next trick is deciding how to

Same family, different flower: the gladioli in the main picture (below) are an old-fashioned species, G. byzantinus, with delicate flowers and a wild look which suits the cottage garden style; whereas a modern hybrid (left) would look out of place with its huge red blooms.

out of hand. The main chores include snipping off dead flowers and cutting back dead or dying stems, pruning, feeding and watering (especially if you have plants in containers) and mulching between plants with garden compost.

The reason for snipping back (deadheading) the dead flowers is to encourage further

put them together, making pleasant contrasts of shape, texture and colour throughout the summer.

A typical small cottage border in a fairly sunny situation might, for instance, contain some old-fashioned roses, lavender, irises, several different kinds of hardy cranesbills, a few salvias and perhaps some summer flowering bulbs like allium or lilies.

For late summer and early autumn flowers, there might

also be a clump or two of Japanese anemones and some Michaelmas daisies.

Roses and honeysuckle make an attractive partnership and, next to them, you could plant night-scented stock or nicotiana for truly wonderful perfumed evenings.

Easy maintenance

Cottage gardens need little work to maintain: just some sensible clearing from time to time when things start getting

Bumble-bees (inset), along with other nectar-loving insects, will be keen visitors to a flower-filled garden of 'wild' species.

flowering. A plant's purpose in life is to flower, set seed, then die. If you take off the dead flowers before they can seed, you are, in effect, frustrating this course of events, and forcing the plant to try again with new flowers.

If you grow tall flowers, like delphiniums, they will need tying loosely and unobtrusively to canes or stakes to keep their stems straight, but most cottage flowers look more natural if they flop gently.

An Evergreen Garden

A garden based on evergreens remains leafy and lush, sheltered and private all year round and you can still have all the colour and seasonal interest you want.

A garden filled with evergreens retains its beauty 12 months a year and can be every bit as interesting as a conventional mixed garden. No longer will you be plagued by falling leaves, never again will your garden look disappointing and bare from autumn until mid-spring.

Evergreen gardens are ideal wherever privacy and the screening off of unpleasant views are important considerations. Many town gardens are hampered by shade. This does not pose a problem for evergreens, many of which thrive in shady spots. Combining some well chosen evergreens with white-painted trellis work is an effective way to enliven a dark basement area. Because urban gardens are often small, every bit of space counts and the many dwarf varieties of evergreen are especially valuable.

Going green!

Suburban gardens also benefit from the screening and privacy that dense evergreen planting can provide, from the typical evergreen boundary hedge to shrubberies. Generous-sized gardens can have an evergreen 'garden within a garden', or magnificent evergreens, such as eucalyptus, cedar of Lebanon or even evergreen magnolia if it is grown near a wall for protection.

Evergreens can range from

This magnificent garden (right) shows that evergreens need not be green. Thuja plicata 'Collyer's Gold', and pink and white heathers add vibrant colour.

53

tiny ground-covering plants a few centimetres high to huge forest trees; from perfectly hardy to tender; and from easy-going, slow-growing plants that more or less look after themselves to plants which need regular pruning, or protection against winter cold or summer drought. Some, such as the rock rose, are short lived, while others, such as evergreen oak, live for hundreds of years.

Suit the site

Try to match your choice of plants to the conditions in your garden. Rhododendrons and camellias, for example, need cool, acid or neutral soil; spotted laurel tolerates deep shade, while senecio and clematis need sun to thrive.

The speed of growth and ultimate size should be considered, especially with conifers, some of which remain dwarf and others, such as Leyland cypress (× *Cupressocyparis*

For beautifully shaped leaves and bright colour as well go for Choisya ternata 'Sundance' (above). Its delicate flowers resemble orange blossom which explains its common name – Mexican orange blossom. The petals are sweetly scented and the leaves, when crushed, release a wonderful aroma.

A more robust looking plant, Vinca major 'Variegata' (above right) grows to 30–60cm/1–2ft but will spread to as much as 1.2m/4ft. The glossy green leaves have gold edges, and pale-blue flowers appear in spring and autumn.

There is no need to plant the whole garden with evergreens, just a small area will do. A large bed by the side of a house (left) has been converted to wonderful effect. These evergreens have been selected to provide maximum contrasts in colour, texture, height and shape and many of the evergreens are fragrant.

GARDENING GLOSSARY

● **Evergreen:** woody stemmed plants that carry leaves throughout the year. (Some perennial, soft-stemmed plants, though, such as Christmas rose, *Helleborus niger*, are also evergreen.) Evergreens do shed their leaves, but only a few at a time and over a long period, so there is never a noticeable change. In most cases their leaves do not change colour, though *Cryptomeria japonica* turns an attractive red shade in autumn.

● **Semi-evergreen:** plants that usually keep their leaves in mild winters, but lose them in severe ones.

● **Deciduous:** plants, usually woody stemmed, whose leaves lose their green colouring and turn orange, red or brown before they are shed at the end of a growing season – generally in autumn. Most herbaceous perennials, such as delphinium and paeony, are also deciduous.

leylandii), quickly outgrow their position. Always check the plant label before buying, and if in doubt ask for advice. Many broad-leaved evergreens, such as cherry laurel and holly are potentially large, but can be kept compact by regular pruning.

Fabulous foliage

'Evergreen' is an umbrella term that includes non-green foliage, from white, yellow, pink, orange and red variegations to palest silver-blue, blue-grey, burgundy and nearly black. Because colourful evergreens are increasingly popular, nurseries bring out stunning new varieties all the time: the recently introduced, bright-yellow Choisya 'Sundance' is just one example.

Variegated evergreens enliven any garden and are especially effective in shade. Variegations usually consist of yellow or white stripes, edges or central splashes to green

Evergreens can be chosen for a variety of features – attractive foliage colour, interesting shapes, berries or textured bark to name but a few. This Daboecia contabrica 'Alba', (left) a member of the heather family, is grown for its beautiful bell-shaped, white flowers. The flowers last from late spring to mid-autumn.

The Ilex aquifolium 'Bacciflava' (right) is common holly which is grown for its wonderful red berries. Both male and female plants are needed if you want berries. This particular variety is covered in dense clusters of vivid yellow berries.

leaves, but sometimes, as in ajuga 'Rainbow' they can be multicoloured.

Many evergreens, such as some heathers, the conifer *Cryptomeria japonica* and the carpeting barrenwort, have foliage that turns attractive red or russet shades in autumn and remains colourful through winter, until the warm spring weather. Others, such as pieris, have young spring growth in attractively contrasting colours. 'Evergreen' also includes 'evergrey', such as senecio 'Sunshine', as beautiful in winter as in summer.

Evergreen foliage ranges from lacy, delicate rue to sword-like New Zealand flax and huge, hand-shaped fatsia. Some evergreen leaves are glossy and reflect the light; others, such as *Viburnum rhytidophyllum*, are mat and velvety. By including a variety of foliage colours, shapes, sizes and textures, you will bring interest to your garden.

PROJECT — AN EVERGREEN TRIO

To enliven a shady corner plant some yellow and green ivy plants 30cm/1ft away from the wall, at 1.2m/4ft spacings, with support canes. Plant variegated *Aucuba japonica* 60cm/2ft away from the corner and a semi-circular clump of *Bergenia cordifolia* in front for a splash of pink.

Camellias and rhododendrons, two of the most popular flowering shrubs, are evergreen, with an immense range of flower colours. Their flowering seasons stretch from late autumn to early summer. Other favourite flowering evergreens include Californian lilac (ceanothus) with its clear blue flowers; escallonia and berberis, both excellent for rambling hedges. There are even evergreen climbing roses.

Everlasting scent

As well as floral fragrance, such as the delicious lemon scent of evergreen magnolias, some evergreen leaves, such as rosemary and thyme, are pleasantly aromatic. The most popular berrying shrubs are also evergreen: holly, cotoneaster and pyracantha. Their berries range from white to yellow, orange and red; *Pernettya mucronata*, a hardy evergreen, provides huge,

marble-like berries in white, pink and purple.

Lastly, though technically deciduous, certain shrubs, such as broom and winter jasmine have bright green stems, creating a lasting effect and contrasting with the more rounded shapes of the leaves.

Mixed options

You could create a very beautiful garden using only evergreens, such as heathers, dwarf conifers or rhododendrons. Or why not select a mixture of shrubs — camellias, hollies, viburnums and laurels. If that sounds too limiting, add more seasonal colour, say from springtime bulbs: tulips, daffodils and hyacinths; biennials: forget-me-nots; wallflowers and and summer bedding plants: petunias and lobelias.

Evergreen plants could provide a framework for beds and borders. They could also fill

The Camellia reticulata (above) has delicate pink, cup-shaped blooms that appear from February until April. The shrub grows to 3–4.5m/10–15ft.

An evergreen border has been planted up (left) with a careful eye to design. There are low growing, dome shaped, and traditional conifers, heathers for colour and berries for seasonal interest.

Grown for its long lasting, fleshy fruits this pink pernettya (below) provides an original centrepiece for any evergreen garden.

pots, tubs, hanging baskets and window boxes to add interest after short-lived flowers have finished. Or leave enough space between evergreen shrubs and trees to tuck in small, temporary groupings for seasonal colour.

If you want the benefits of evergreens, but still have your heart set on such favourites as flowering cherry and lilac simply increase the number of evergreens in your garden. As old plants die, replace them with evergreens, that way, you will create a well-balanced, foliage-filled garden that requires less work.

A Water Garden

A water feature enhances any garden, and provides a home for a host of attractive plants, both in the water and around its edges.

Water is an important element in garden design, beautiful in itself. The tinkle of running water, whether it plays from a fountain or falls from a ledge, has a soothing, relaxing effect, while a still pool reflects the colours and moods of the sky and clouds and sends shafts of sunlight dancing across the garden.

Water is also a growing medium for plants. Whether you have a formal pool complete with fountain, a small stream, or a sprawling, naturalistic pond, the right choice of plants can enhance its beauty. Even a stubbornly soggy patch in a forgotten corner of the garden can be made a feature.

Wild life

A well-planted water garden also makes an attractive environment for a host of interesting and colourful insects, amphibians and fish.

Brightly-coloured damsel flies and dragonflies hover and flutter across the surface and cling to the leaves, while pond-skaters dart across the limpid water.

Frogs, toads and newts will quickly colonize a pond, producing masses of spawn in the spring and helping to keep the slug population down.

Fish will, of course, have to be introduced, unless you are lucky enough to have a stream flowing through the garden. Goldfish will feed on spawn and tadpoles, but so will native fish, and even cats! There is no need to exclude them on wildlife grounds, and their darting, sun-gold presence near the surface in warm weather is always a boon.

Birds also enjoy visiting ponds, both for drinking and bathing. They need shallow water for this, so make sure there is a ledge or a gentle slope at at least one place in the pond that they can use. Frogs, toads and newts also require this sort of access point if they are to get in and out of the water easily.

Plants naturally increase the wild life potential of a water feature; their flowers attract insects while their leaves and stems make perches for them, as well as offering shade and shelter at the water's edge for birds and amphibians.

Some plants perform special

Even a small pool can be home to a number of attractive flowering and foliage plants (above). Here, a small, non-classical statue provides a focus in a basically informal design incorporating lilies and several marginal plants.

Marginals can be planted according to the same principles as a bed (right). A variegated grass gives height and water mint (Mentha aquatica) dark, aromatic leaves. A monkey flower (Mimulus luteus) provides yellow flowers, and water forget-me-not (Myosotis scorpioides), blue ones.

There are many ways of bringing a small pond to life with summer colour. One traditional solution is to plant one or two varieties from the enormous water lily genus; Nymphaea 'Froebelii' (right) adds to the appeal of its flowers with mottled leaves. The appeal of water lilies is enhanced by stocking your pond with ornamental fish. Goldfish or koi carp (above) swim close to the surface on warm days, flashing gold and silver in the sunshine, and, providing the pond is not too shallow, can survive weeks of icy weather in the winter.

tasks, cleaning and oxygenating the water to improve the environment, or preventing the build up of algae, the primitive, microscopic plants that discolour the water, and make a green slick over pebbles and other surfaces.

The ripple effect

There are plants to suit all watery environments: deep or shallow water; pond margins, swamp or wet land.

You can create a succession of bands of plants, according to the amount of moisture they like around their roots. These bands move out from the deep centre of the pond like the ripples made by a stone thrown into a pool. Each ripple performs an important function, as well as providing colour and ornament to the design.

Plants that live in the centre of the pond are known as deep-water aquatics. They root at the bottom of the pond, either in planting crates or in a layer of soil, while their leaves and flowers float at, or just above, the surface.

The best-known deep-water aquatics are the water lilies (*Nymphaea spp.*). Hybridiz-

PLANTING TIMES

Plant water gardens in spring and early summer. Warmer water, rising air temperatures and longer hours of daylight all encourage strong growth.

If you've just filled a pool with water, let it stand for up to ten days to allow the chlorine in tap water to evaporate.

GROWING TIPS

The yellow and white flower spikes and blue-green leaves of the aquatic, golden club (Orontium aquaticum), *make it an ornament to any pond (below). It is a spring-flowering perennial which requires full sun to flourish.*

ation has created a range of varieties to suit anyone's taste or the size of their pond.

Excellent alternatives include the water hawthorn (*Aponogeton distachyus*) whose small white flowers have a scent like hawthorn blossom, and the golden club (*Orontium aquaticum*), which produces long, yellow and white flower spikes.

Most of these plants have large, flat leaves that are attractive in themselves but also provide good shade, preventing the growth of algae.

The breath of life

Every still pond needs oxygenating plants if it is to support a wide variety of life. Like deep-water aquatics, oxygenating plants have their roots and stems submerged. The difference is that their leaves are under water, too.

This means that they aerate the water, keeping it clear. All plants produce oxygen as a by-product of converting sunlight into food and respire it through their leaves; oxygen-

Among the most attractive marginal plants is the flowering rush (Butomus umbellatus). *Its twisting green leaves give height at the side of a pond, but it is grown mainly for its heads of pink and red summer flowers (above).*

Marginals can be planted in the soil at the water's edge, but they are easier to handle – and much easier to lift for thinning out or division – if they are planted in perforated plastic baskets specially designed for the purpose (right).

ating plants release it directly into the water, rather than into the atmosphere.

This is a bonus for fish, which breathe the oxygen, although in shaded or overcast conditions the oxygen is produced at a much slower rate.

The underwater foliage provides shelter, nutrients and breeding grounds for fish and newts. It also has a vital preventative function. The leaves absorb mineral nutrients from the water, depriving algae of vital foods.

Many oxygenating plants are decorative as well as useful. The water starwort (*Callitriche verna* syn *C. palustris*) has feathery, divided leaves

Most water lilies require room to spread. The sweetly-scented Nymphaea 'Odorata Alba' (above) is an exception, however, flourishing in relatively small pools.

Those lucky enough to have a stream running through, or at the end of, their garden, will find that they can clothe its banks with the many colourful garden plants that appreciate moist soil (left). Here, the flower-heads of various species of achillea combine with rock roses (Helianthemum spp.), monkey flowers (Mimulus spp.), the mat-forming speedwell (Veronica prostrata) and others to make a wonderful summer display.

that swirl into attractive shapes just below the surface, and carries its delicate flowers high above the water, while water milfoil (*Myriophyllum spicatum*) has red-tipped, feathery foliage.

Be sure to avoid invasive oxygenating plants such as Canadian pondweed (*Elodea canadensis*). Goldfish weed (*Elodea crispa*) is an attractive, non-rampant alternative.

Floating plants

Many water plants do not need to root in soil at all. Instead, they float across the pond, pushed by winds and the movement of water wildlife.

Fairy moss (*Azolla caroliniana*) is a tiny plant that spreads quickly to form a dense mat. In spring, it is coloured a fresh green: in autumn it turns russet-red. It tends to be invasive, but it is easy enough to control in a small pond, as you can simply

The cheery yellow flowers of the flag (Iris pseudacorus), *held aloft on stems as much as 1.5m/5ft tall – though usually a little less – brighten up a pondside. The yellow leaf stripes of 'Variegata' (left) fade after the plant flowers in early to mid summer.*

FERTILIZERS

Special aquatic fertilizer with a high phosphate content is available. It is slowly released throughout the growing season. Don't use ordinary fertilizer or manure as these rapidly dissolve and will boost algal growth.

GARDEN NOTES

You do not need a lot of space or a sprawling informal pond to house a good selection of water plants (above). In this patio, a pond has been created by building up the sides rather than digging, and a raised central area allows for the planting of aquatics that require different depths of water in which to flourish.

IMPROVING A BOG

If your bog garden is on a clay or heavy soil that holds water too well in winter and loses it spectacularly in summer, when it bakes to a brick-hard consistency, your moisture-loving bog garden plants will die.

To lighten and improve the drainage, work in well-rotted organic matter and mulch around the plant roots after watering it thoroughly.

If the soil is light and sandy, create a boggy patch by digging an area near the pond, covering it with a piece of pond-liner and filling with organic matter and soil. Flood it when you top up the pond, and you will be able to plant it up with moisture-loving plants.

GO ORGANIC!

lift out any excessive growth with a fine-meshed net.

Like deep-water aquatics, floating plants are excellent at controlling algae. The floating mats of leaves move across the water, soaking up the sunlight the algae need.

Marginals

Marginal plants such as rushes and flags (yellow water irises) grow at the edges of ponds. They like to have their roots in shallow water – from 5-30cm/2-12in – or, like the dwarf Japanese rush (*Acorus gramineus* 'Variegatus'), at water level.

When marginal plants are well-established they soften the edges of a pond, hiding plastic liners or other obtrusive, structural features. They also provide shelter for emerging froglets and for birds.

Otherwise, marginals are purely decorative. Most of them have an upright habit, providing a strong vertical emphasis against the horizontal surface of the pond. Many also have fine flowers, such as the marsh marigold (*Caltha palustris*), which produces a brilliant profusion of yellow flowers in spring, the flowering rush (*Butomus umbellatus*), whose small rose-pink flowers wave from tall, elegant stems, and the yellow flag (*Iris pseudacorus*).

Some plants enjoy growing

A bog area makes a good home for many moisture-loving decorative plants (above). Here, the grassy foliage of a sedge and the spreading leaves of a hosta provide the background for the feathery pink flowers of astilbe.

The mimulus genus has produced a number of modern hybrid varieties, much showier than the species, with the yellow flowers heavily speckled with red. Many can flourish in a border, but all look best at the margins of a pond (below).

in the permanently soggy conditions around the edges of an informal pool, and can be used to bridge the gap between the pond and the planting in rest of the garden.

This is particulary true of those such as *Astilbe* spp., bugle (*Ajuga reptans*) and plantain lilies (*Hosta* spp.), all of which also grow happily in other parts of the garden.

Some waterside plants are tall-growing or large-leaved and will provide dramatic focal points. If you have the space, giant rhubarb (*Gunnera manicata*) gives you a mound of huge, spreading rhubarb-type leaves and a tall central flower spike.

Finishing touch

To complete the ripple effect of your water garden planting, add a tree or two. Many trees grow naturally in wet conditions, and will make a graceful backdrop to a wild-life water garden or at the top of a bank.

Willow and birch are full of year-round interest, with attractive bark and outlines in winter, catkins in spring, and foliage in summer and autumn. Do not plant trees too close, however; they cast shade and fallen leaves will pollute the water.

A Touch of Formality

Introduce a touch of formality into your plot, no matter what its size. Whether you choose simply to add a statue or to transform your whole garden, here are some great ideas to get you started.

If you wish to create a garden that is well ordered and neat, with straight paths and formal flower beds, a tidy patio and a well-trimmed lawn – perhaps with a statue, bird bath or other decoration – then the classic ornamental garden is the right kind for you.

Whether planning your garden from scratch or making changes to your existing plot, do not make the mistake of considering the garden in isolation. Your design should also take into account the architecture of your home. An intricate design would look out of place next to a simple, modern house, for example.

Perfect symmetry

The overall effect you are looking for in an ornamental garden is one of clean, simple, uncluttered lines. Beds, borders, patios, lawns and other features need to be geometric in shape. They also need to form part of an overall symmetry.

In your quest for a harmonious design, no element should be left 'out on a limb'. Your geometric-shaped flower-beds, for example, should be incorporated into the patio or lawn, or surrounded by neat paths.

Formal beds need formal planting. In spring, a carpet of forget-me-nots, polyanthus or wallflowers punctuated regularly with bedding tulips could be used. The bed could be

An ornamental garden need not be complicated in its design: this garden (left) is all the more pleasing for its simplicity. A pair of lemon trees in pots flank the doorway and a single terracotta urn provides an eye-catching central feature.

If you feel that a statue would be too grand for your garden, why not have a bird bath instead? This one (left) has been placed in the middle of a circular lawn. The round shapes of lawn and bowl are further echoed by the brick-edged bed at the base of the pedestal. As well as being a decorative feature in its own right, a bird bath will also attract birds to your garden.

small number of plants and colours. Go for single colours instead of mixtures when choosing bedding plants and aim to harmonize the beds with the colour of the house, paths, walls and fences.

Low levels

A classic ornamental feature worth considering is a sunken garden. These are usually square or rectangular and the depth should be in proportion

A BEAUTIFUL LAWN

An untidy lawn can ruin the effect of an ornamental garden. If yours is a mess, do not despair. Rather than dig it up and start again, there are ways you can improve it.
● mow regularly and frequently to discourage the growth of coarse rye grasses and encourage finer grasses
● as well as regular cutting, feed frequently with a proprietary fertilizer
● to discourage moss, aerate the lawn in dry conditions and, if soil is acid, add lime
● after aerating, add a top dressing of sharp sand and rake it in
● children and dogs can damage the lawn, so if you really want it to look beautiful, don't allow them to play on the grass or it might end up looking like a football pitch!

GROWING TIPS

edged broadly with a border of double daisies. If you have a group of formal beds, you could stick to the same scheme in each one or different, complementary plantings.

For summer, there are so many bedding plants from which to make your selection that there is an almost infinite variety of combinations.

The right plants

Effective schemes include a carpet of wax begonias or zonal pelargoniums punctuated with silver-leaved *Senecio bicolor*, with a centrepiece of tall cabbage palm (*Cordyline australis*). Remember, however, that these plants are not hardy enough to grow reliably out of doors unless you live in a mild or sheltered area.

Choose plants to suit your own particular climate and soil conditions, following a few simple style guidelines. For an uncluttered effect stick to a

PERFECT PARTNERS

It is best to keep to simple colour schemes in your ornamental garden – a mixture of hues could detract from the orderliness of the design. Here, the white tulip 'Pax' has been combined with 'Crystal Bowl' pansies.

When it comes to deciding on plants to fill your ornamental garden, the choice is huge – but there are some that seem especially 'right' for this style of design. Plants to go for are those that are tidy and echo the orderliness of your design.

Taller plants with straight, upright stems such as tulips can look very effective placed in a sea of neat, low-growing flowers such as pansies. The impressive crown imperial (*Fritillaria imperialis*) can be used in a similar way. When combining different plants, check that their flowering times are the same.

For a traditional touch, why not try a pair of standard roses, placed symmetrically in your design? Surround them with one of the more compact forms of lavender, such as Dutch lavender (*Lavandula vera*).

Many herbs are ideal plants for the ornamental garden, forming neat clumps and having the added appeal of aromatic foliage and a practical use in the kitchen, too. Combine blue-grey sage, golden balm and parsley.

AN 'ANTIQUE' CONTAINER

A new concrete container can look too bright and clean but by the clever application of a little paint you can easily 'age' it to blend in with its surroundings. Getting the exact shade you want is a matter of trial and error: what you are aiming for is a natural-looking stone colour. Do a test on a piece of scrap paper first.

This method can also be used for 'antiquing' plastic containers – but omit the last stage as sanding is likely to make the paint flake off.

You will need:
raw umber acrylic paint
black acrylic paint
white emulsion paint
2 paintbrushes
medium glass paper

1 *Assemble your materials before you begin. You can paint more than one container at a time.*

2 *Pour some emulsion into a jar and add small amount of raw umber acrylic paint. Paint the container.*

3 *Add more raw umber and dab on paint allowing the lighter base colour to show through.*

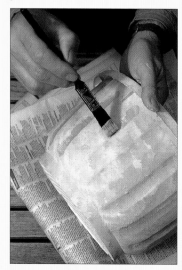

4 *Add some black paint to your mixture and paint the hollow parts, softening edges with a dry brush.*

5 *When the paint is dry, rub over the paint surface with glass paper to give a 'distressed' finish.*

BALANCING ACT

Two of the key things to watch out for when planning your ornamental garden are *symmetry* and *balance* – which simply means you should aim to get an equal balance between the different parts on opposite sides of the garden, borders or paths. A tall plant on one side should be matched by a similar plant, or ornament, on the other; a wide border could be balanced by a wide path. Neat, geometric shapes are also the right ones for your beds, paths and ponds.

to the area: the smaller the garden, the shallower it should be. Do not scale down your sunken garden too much, however. It should form a major part of the overall design of your ornamental garden. One possibility is to let it span the width of a narrow plot, creating a split-level effect. Changes of level will add an exciting new dimension to the look of your garden. As a guide, the depth should be about 30-60cm/12-24in.

Decorative details

The low retaining walls of your sunken garden can be built up with bricks. Ideally these should match the house, or be made from decorative concrete walling blocks.

For a really splendid effect, add a central feature such as a statue, sundial, most impressive of all, a small formal pool with a fountain.

Generally this is a wedge shape, broader at the base than at the top, with a rounded or flat top – but you can choose whichever shape you please, of course.

Hedges can also be used within the garden, to divide it into a number of areas. Separate the formal from the informal part of the garden if you have enough space.

Formal hedges should be 1.8m/6ft max. in height and will need regular clipping in the growing season to keep them in shape and prevent them from growing too tall.

Classic features

Low box hedges are an element in another classic formal garden feature, the *parterre*. This consists of geometric beds arranged in a regular pattern and set in a gravel area with space to walk between. The beds are edged with low hedges of dwarf box (*Buxus sempervirens* 'Suffruticosa'), which must be clipped regularly for a neat finish. The beds can be filled with seasonal bedding or, if you want a more subtle, all-green look, with low-growing culinary and ornamental herbs.

Choosing accessories to dress up your formal garden is probably the most enjoyable part. Make your selection from the array of statues, sundials and ornamental containers you will find on display at most large garden centres.

Finishing touches

Use ornaments in moderation, as it is all too easy to go too far and ruin the simple, elegant effect you are aiming for. If space is limited, a well-chosen piece situated in the corner of the patio, beside a pool or at the far end of the lawn will be more effective than lots of little objects scattered all over the garden.

A statue is a good choice as a focal point, to draw the eye to a particular part of the garden. If you decide to put a statue in your garden, choose one that matches the scale of your plot. Avoid using a life-sized human figure if you have a pocket-

Your sunken garden can be laid out with geometric beds set in gravel or paving and planted with seasonal bedding, or you could create a formal rose garden.

A sunken rose garden can consist of a single bed or a group of geometric beds, perhaps set in a gravel or paved area or in a lawn. Choose formal roses such as large-flowered (hybrid tea) or cluster-flowered (floribunda) varieties. For tiny gardens, scale things down by using miniature roses.

Plant one variety per bed, perhaps with a standard rose, ideally of the same variety, in the centre of each bed, to give additional height.

Hedging bets

The boundaries of a formal ornamental garden are usually planted with formal hedges trained to a regular shape.

Statuary is very much part of the ornamental garden style. A well-placed statue can provide a bold focal point, leading the eye to a particular corner, and can form an essential part of the design. The circular area of gravel (above) cries out for some form of ornament to mark its centre: without the little trumpeter in the middle, it would have seemed very bare. The small figure holds the design together.

In another garden (right), cleverly placed urns and round paving slabs lead the eye naturally across the gravelled area to the statue on the far side. The dark, evergreen hedge behind it provides the perfect foil, accentuating the figure's form.

handkerchief-sized garden; a bust might be better, perhaps set on a pedestal or on a wall of a raised bed. Human figures and busts are suited to virtually any garden; those that are naked or carrying a vessel are

probably most appropriate near water. If you have a pond, you may also like to consider placing a stone frog, fish or heron by the side of it.

If your statue is light in colour, set it against a dark background such as a hedge or brick wall. Set it next to a formal shrub such as a bay or fatsia, or soften its outlines with a climbing plant.

Modern wood

For an ultra-modern garden, you may prefer to choose a geometric object: a stone obelisk, pyramid, cube or sphere. Use a pair to flank a path or gateway, or place a single object so that it adds drama to a plain lawn or paved area.

A sundial mounted on a pedestal makes a good centrepiece for a sunken bed or the

In the restrained elegance of the ornamental garden, one of the pleasures you can enjoy is variety in colour and texture – and there are plenty of combinations to choose from. Here (left) the deep red of Begonia semperflorens contrasts with the yellow of Helichrysum petiolare 'Aureum' or 'Limelight'.

centre of a lawn. A container such as a stone urn can perform a similar function, while containers which are set in groups – ideally of similar design but not of the same size – can look extremely elegant.

Containers come in all shapes and sizes. A square wooden Versailles tub looks good in most settings and can be painted to match your

GROWING TIPS

FORMAL HEDGES

These evergreen trees and shrubs are ideal for creating a boundary:
- box (*Buxus sempervirens*) is moderately slow-growing and needs frequent clipping, but forms a good, dense hedge
- Lawson cypress (*Chamaecyparis lawsoniana*) 'Green Hedger' is fast-growing and needs only annual clipping
- holly (*Ilex aquifolium*) is slow-growing, but dense if clipped regularly
- yew (*Taxus baccata*) is moderately slow-growing, but becomes very dense with regular clipping
- western red cedar (*Thuja plicata* 'Atrovirens') is a fast grower with fruity aromatic foliage and needs only annual trimming

cotta which creates a 'warm', rather rustic effect, and may be better suited to more informal parts of the garden. The most stylish – and expensive – garden ornaments are made of stone, but reconstituted stone makes a good substitute. A decorative stone urn can be left unplanted and placed on a matching pedestal to grace a paved area or the centre of a rose garden.

Formal containers are best planted with neat, formal-looking plants – a mass of flowers and greenery tumbling

house. Rounded urns, vases and jars make good focal points, say at the end of a lawn, or as centrepieces for formal rose or sunken gardens. Containers also come in various different materials. At the cheaper end of the range, there is concrete and plastic. These materials may be cheap but in the long run they may be a false economy. Remember

The still surface of this rectangular pond (above left) is uncluttered by plants and calmly reflects the sky. This well-coordinated scheme (above right) has yellow Tagetes 'Lemon Gem' around the edge, with white begonias 'Silver Devil' and a single Artemisia 'Powis Castle' in the middle.

that your garden ornaments may be with you for years, and you may later regret not having splashed out a little more in the beginning to get something that is better quality and continues to be attractive.

Stylish stone

Next in the price range is glass-reinforced cement, a very presentable material, and terra-

loosely over the sides could spoil the tidy effect you have been working to achieve. Good choices would be clipped bay trees or perhaps some topiary in box or yew. You could even try a citrus tree, although if you live in one of the colder areas of the country you would need to bring this indoors into a greenhouse or a conservatory for the winter.

A Wildlife Haven

By creating a haven for wildlife, you can turn your garden into a living landscape full of the incandescent colours of birds and butterflies.

Loss of habitat as a result of intensive farming and land development is becoming a cause for concern to naturalists and amateur nature-lovers alike. By making your garden environmentally friendly, you can help to redress the balance and preserve the beautiful and fascinating natural world around you.

Recently, gardeners have started to take a far greater interest in the natural world on their doorsteps. We have become better informed. A deeper understanding of the importance of habitat has led to a move towards organic gardening methods. Creatures that were once seen as unwanted pests are now viewed with more benevolent eye as vital links in the food chain.

Good news

The good news is that by creating a wildlife haven you can add whole new dimensions to your garden. The gentle hum of insects and the lyrical songs of birds add a soothing counterpoint to the visual aspects of the garden.

Insects such as butterflies will add yet more colour to your flower beds and borders. The darting, fluttering, floating and scuttling of birds and insects gives movement in the air and on the ground.

It is not just a question of throwing a much-needed lifeline to some endangered species but also about encouraging and nurturing those which are not struggling. After all, effective prevention is far better than cure.

By making your garden friendly to wildlife, you will

have the deep satisfaction of 'doing good' and the added bonus of creating a sanctuary of breathtaking beauty for you and your family.

If you have children, your garden will become a living classroom. It will teach them to love and respect the natural world and to protect and preserve it in their turn.

Whether you are starting from scratch or intend to adapt an existing garden, you will need to make a plan.

A lot will depend on the size of the area you are working with and the needs of you and your family. Begin by drawing a sketch of your garden showing fixed features, patio area, shed and so on.

Nectar-rich flowers like umbellifers attract hoverflies (above). The darting, hovering flight of these insects makes them attractive, and they also have a practical use. Their young feed on aphids; each larva accounts for around 600 of these garden pests as it matures.

70

Next, make a list of possible habitats such as a pond, meadowland, woodland, rocky outcrop and hedgerow. Bear in mind that a woodland habitat need not be the size of a small forest and that a serviceable meadow need be no larger than an average lawn. Go back to your plan and see how many habitats you can realistically fit into the space available.

A wildlife garden need not be a wilderness. Many 'wild' habitats are, in fact, managed. Woodlands or hedgerows, for example, both require regular maintenance. A formal setting can be just as inviting to wildlife as an informal one.

You will be astonished at what you already provide for

One of the most time-honoured ways of attracting wildlife to your garden is to provide a bird table. Several birds such as starlings (above) will appreciate a supplement to their winter diet, especially when snow and ice make natural food difficult to obtain. A less obvious environment is beneath a stone. Digging out a small hole beneath a stepping stone (above, right) will provide a roomy shelter for a frog, for instance. However, the main way to provide for wildlife in the garden is by sympathetic planting. Even a wall can be made an important food source if it is well planted (right). Here, the structure of the wall has all but disappeared beneath a flowery blanket of erigeron, nepeta, aubrieta, cerastium and hypericum.

CARING FOR BIRDS

Most gardeners like to feed the birds, especially in winter when times are hard. The food you supply should include seeds, nuts, fats (animal or vegetable), fruit and preferably wholemeal bread. Remember to supply water for drinking and bathing. Phase out feeding in spring when natural food supplies are plentiful. Begin again in autumn.

If you want birds to take up residence in your garden then nest sites are essential. A good thick hedge or a selection of trees are ideal. Bird boxes are fine but must be strategically placed. A good bird book will give you the information you need.

You can encourage house-martins to nest by supplying the mud with which they build. Dig a shallow hollow, line it with polythene and place earth on top. Water regularly to keep it moist.

Don't Forget!

wildlife. Seemingly barren areas such as a wall or a patio may already be home to a variety of insects and other creatures. A few simple measures can help to encourage even more to take up residence.

Stepping stones across your lawn could become home to frogs and toads, for example. Dig out a shallow depression about 4cm/1½in deep and supply a small corridor rising up to ground level. Pop your stepping stone over the top, leaving the entrance to the corridor just visible in the grass. Even if you don't have a pond, you may still get visitors, especially if there is a pond in the vicinity.

Bountiful boundaries

Walls and fences provide all sorts of benefits for wildlife. They correspond to rock faces or banks in the wild, and make admirable perches for birds and pupating sites for moths and butterflies without any work from you.

You can enhance their attractiveness as a garden feature and as a wildlife habitat by clothing them with plants. There are many plants that

A birdbath can be incorporated into a design as an ornamental feature (above). Remember, though, that birds are vulnerable when bathing or drinking. It is prudent to site a birdbath away from any features where a predatory cat might lurk waiting to pounce.

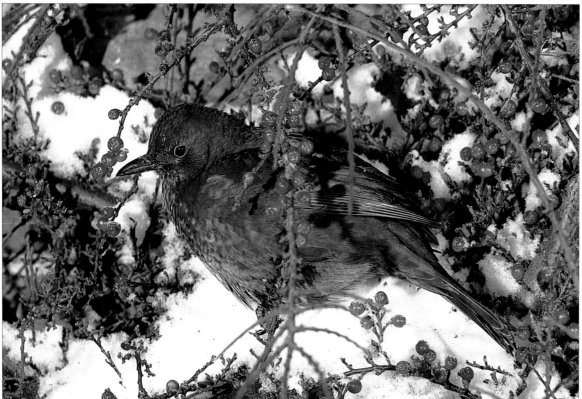

Plants which carry plenty of berries are just as important a winter food source for birds in the garden as the seed and scraps left for them on the bird table. Birds which normally survive on worms or insects, such as blackbirds (left) or other members of the thrush family, will gladly take berries in the depths of winter.

will grow happily in, on or against a wall. *Senecio greyi*, an upright shrub when grown in a border, can be grown against a wall where it provides dense, protective foliage as it drapes itself decorously over the top. Various alpines are only too pleased to settle in crevices, although it is best to plant these as you build.

Honeysuckle is vigorous and full of nectar and pollen during its flowering season. Its fragrance is an added delight.

The common wild ivy (*Hedera helix*) is one of the best all-purpose wildlife garden plants. The nectar-rich flowers which appear in late autumn on mature plants attract a multitude of insects, including the odd butterfly stocking up for hibernation. Birds roost and make nests in it and its protective foliage welcomes

The green flowers which appear on mature ivy plants in autumn are a valuable food source for those insects which have not yet gone into hibernation. Several butterflies, such as the comma, painted lady and red admiral (right) take its nectar.

Tits are basically woodland birds, feeding on insects in the summer and seeds in the autumn and winter. They are also extremely fond of peanuts. Specially-designed feeders, hung from a convenient tree branch, encourage the birds to show off their gymnastic and aerobatic skills (below). Here, two blue tits (on left), a great tit (lower right) and a coal tit (upper right) have flown in for a feast.

many hibernating creatures, including butterflies.

A warm, sunny, dry stone wall, full of nooks and crannies, is the perfect place for slow worms. These legless lizards are excellent for controlling slugs and other pests. If your wall is brick and mortar, simply chipping out the cement here and there may make it more attractive proposition, not only for slow worms, but for various insects and pupating moths and butterflies as well.

Hedgerows

If you are lucky enough to have a natural hedge made up of native plants such as hawthorn, blackthorn, field maple (*Acer campestre*) and wild privet, count your blessing and hang on to it. If you are planning to plant one, then consider using these species in preference to conifers and other hedging plants.

Such a hedge will attract as many as 20 species of butterfly, a huge variety of birds and some small mammals. Hedges act as a sort of corridor for wildlife, providing them with protection as they wander. They also provide food, nesting sites and a place to hibernate.

You can enhance your hedge by planting native wild flowers such as red campion, wild arum, bluebells and greater stitchwort at the base.

Paths and patios

When planning your patio and paths, leave room between the flag stones to plant pollen and nectar rich plants such as creeping thyme, aubrieta, chamomile, alyssum, apple mint and forget-me-not. Bees and butterflies will be very grateful for such a rich source of pollen and nectar.

There are several other advantages to planting paths and patios. They soften the outlines of otherwise fairly harsh features and stop less desirable plants from filling in the gaps. Creeping or spreading herbs have the added bonus of surrounding you with

FOOD PLANTS

Several decorative plants provide food for birds in the form of fruit and seeds, as well, of course, as attracting insects on which other birds can feed.

The fruit of ornamental apple and cherry trees is unpalatable to us, but welcome to many birds. Varieties of cotoneaster also produce succulent berries, but avoid *C. conspicuus* 'Decorus'.

The hips of the dog rose (*Rosa canina*) are much prized, as are the berries of the elder (*Sambucus nigra*) and holly (*Ilex aquifolium*).

Birds also enjoy hawthorn (*Crataegus monogyna*), honeysuckle, wild privet (*Ligustrum vulgare*), snapdragons (*Antirrhinum* spp.), evening primrose (*Oenothera* spp.) and sunflower (*Helianthus annuus*).

GARDEN NOTES

The common hawthorn (Crataegus monogyna) is a wonderfully decorative plant in late spring and early summer, when it is in full flower (above). It also produces handsome red berries later in the season. The berries and flowers are an important food source and its twisted, thorny branches provide shelter for nesting birds and pupating insects. It can be grown as a specimen tree, but is perhaps more useful to wildlife as part of a hedge.

No wildlife garden should be without some kind of water feature where birds and animals can drink and bathe. A mature informal pond (left) is the ideal. A mix of native and cultivated plants makes it easy on the eye, as well as providing shelter for drinking animals. Frogs will spawn in a fairly small pond, provided they can get access to it. The common frog (right) is the most likely visitor; it will come to spawn in the spring, and return occasionally in the summer, particularly in hot weather.

Hedgehogs are rarely seen because they do their roaming and hunting at night. They supplement their basic diet of insects, worms, slugs and spiders with fresh carrion, and will gladly take some cat or dog food (above). If, over a period of time, you gradually move the dish nearer the house, they can be encouraged to feed in full view of a window.

fragrance as you sit in the sun or walk your paths.

Water is a vital ingredient in a wildlife garden. A pond is the obvious way of providing it. It needn't be large, as even a tiny pond will support a good selection of life forms.

A good wildlife pond provides a variety of depths. It is best if it slopes gently to a depth of at least 75cm/30in – so it does not freeze solid in winter – with a ledge 30cm/1ft deep at the other end.

If you extend the pond liner beneath the soil you can provide a very desirable wetland area. Remember to provide a hard surface for a viewing point. You don't want to have to wade through bogland to have a close look at the teeming life in your pond.

Some creatures, such as water snails, spend their

HEDGEHOGS

Hedgehogs are the best-loved of our native mammals. They may well be visiting your garden already, as their foraging range is quite large. You can encourage their visits by supplying tasty plates of dog food. Don't be tempted to leave bread and milk for them as it is too rich.

If you wish them to take up residence, you must supply a good place for them to lie up during the day, to hibernate and, with luck, to breed. Underneath the shed is a good place as long as there is plenty of good nesting material such as dry leaves, straw or hay. They also like to nest under a wood pile, with insulation material provided. A weatherproof wooden box, filled with nesting material and placed under a pile of logs and leaves makes a very desirable property for hedgehogs.

whole lives in water. Others are tied to it by their breeding habits; these include frogs, toads and dragonflies. Some move from one pond to another – water boatmen and pond-skaters for example. Others just visit for food, for a bath and of course, to drink.

A wildlife pond requires some planning and it is as well to do your research carefully before investing in a pond liner. One thing to consider is the safety of young children.

If you find it is impossible to make the pond out-of-bounds to the very young, put the project on hold until they are old enough not to drown in it. Meanwhile, a few shallow dishes dotted around your garden will provide birds with the much-needed drinking and bathing facilities.

An elegant birdbath can make an excellent focal point while being immensely useful to birds. Do remember to provide fresh water regularly, especially in winter when other supplies are frozen.

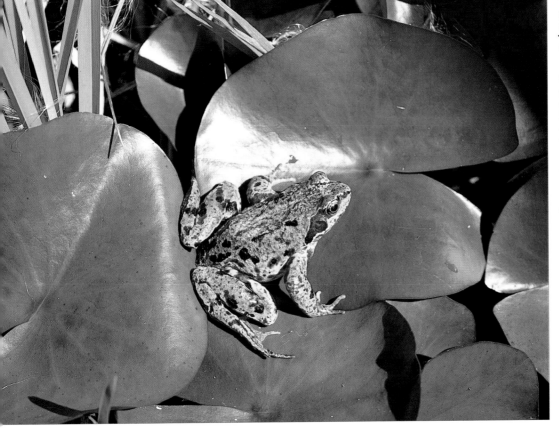

A Mediterranean Garden

Simple alterations – white paint, terracotta pots, gravel and a few exotic plants – can evoke the atmosphere of the sun-drenched Mediterranean in your garden.

White walls and red pantiles, clusters of containers brimming with annuals, sparkling gravel and cool conifers; all these things speak of Mediterranean heat, yet this garden has been created in temperate southern England.

Differences in culture and climate have produced a distinctly different style of gardening around the Mediterranean. It is, though, a style that can, with a few adaptations, be applied in temperate climates. It's not at all difficult to do, and is ideally suited to the small spaces that most of us have nowadays. Or, less ambitiously, you could give just part of your garden the Mediterranean treatment – perhaps the front-of-house area, or the patio.

What exactly is a Mediterranean garden? Individual gardens vary, of course, but as you may know from Continental holidays, they are often quite formal in character, with geometric shapes – square, rectangular or round beds, and straight paths – rather than the undulations and curves usually recommended by British garden designers.

The lawn is conspicuous by its absence, for the purely practical reason that grass does not grow lush and green without lavish amounts of rain – it would be brown for most of the summer. Gravel and paving take the place of grass, allowing paths to be integrated with open areas around the beds and creating a spacious feel even in tiny plots.

Sun traps

Many such gardens are sun traps, enclosed by high white walls, characteristically capped with curved red tiles (pantiles), and often pierced by archways offering tantalizing glimpses of what lies beyond.

Other typical features are masses of pelargoniums, tumbling from a balcony or planted in ornate terracotta pots, small formal pools and fountains, spiky architectural plants like yuccas and phormiums, and column-shaped trees, especially dark cypress, which make dramatic accents against a clear blue sky.

Enclosures

If your garden is walled, or part walled, you are off to a flying start. Paint boundary walls with two or three coats of white exterior grade emulsion, and if possible lay red pantiles along the top – these are available from most builder's merchants.

Unless recently creosoted, fencing can be painted white with water-based paint designed for use on timber. The effect will not be quite the same, but white paint will give you the extra light-reflectance essential for a sunny feel.

Traditional privet hedges are not really in style, but a conifer one, especially if dark, might look just right. If you already have a privet hedge, clip it closely and often for a formal look; if you are feeling particularly ambitious, you could start training it into a

PERFUMED GARDEN

Do not forget to include fragrance in your Mediterranean garden. Plant thyme, marjoram and rosemary, whose scent is redolent of hillsides all over France, Italy and Greece. To get maximum fragrance, put them in a sunny spot backed by heat-retaining paving or rocks.

Choose strongly scented shrubs like lilac, philadelphus and Mexican orange blossom (*Choisya ternata*) and fragrant varieties of rose.

GARDEN NOTES

The right plants can add to the impression of warmth. Hot bright colours – reds, oranges and yellows – are the best choice for bedding plants and annuals. Free-flowering plants such as petunias and pelargoniums, especially when they are displayed against white walls and light gravels, give the best effect (above).

Other suitable container subjects are exotic, succulent plants such as the agaves. This one (left) is 'Variegata', a variety of the century plant (A. americana).

geometric topiary shape.

Another possibility is to create a new wall across the garden to define your Mediterranean area. Use concrete walling blocks, rendered and topped with pantiles, to a height of 1.8m/6ft. For a Spanish look, use decorative pierced blocks.

If you cannot do any of these things, just paint the lower part of the house wall white — fake or real shutters added to the windows add to the Mediterranean look.

Gardens in the Mediterranean are thought of as outdoor rooms, and the authentic look requires furnishing (right). A sunshade is de rigeur, even if not strictly necessary in the local climate.

Scent is as important as colour; the flowers and foliage of Lonicera japonica *'Aureoreticulata' (below) provide both, even in a shady, north-facing spot.*

Gravel has a hot, dry look reminiscent of poor Mediterranean soils and sparkles in the sun. It is also very practical, providing a clean, free-draining surface to walk on at little cost. Choose a pale, neutral-coloured gravel for a natural look and maximum light reflectance.

Provided the soil is treated with weedkiller first, or the gravel laid over polythene, an annual application of path weedkiller should keep it completely weed-free. Lay the gravel at least 5cm/2in thick, to replace grass and to make straight paths and rectangular shapes. Confine it with bricks, edging slabs or timber so that it does not disappear into the surrounding soil.

Paving is more expensive than gravel, but many gardens already have a small paved area at the back of the house, which could be extended. Again, if the paving is informal in shape, relay it in a more formal design.

Some kind of water feature is an essential part of any Mediterranean garden, preferably one including a simple fountain to provide the soothing sound of falling water.

If you already have a pool, and it is the usual natural or kidney shape, remake it in a round, rectangular or octagonal design. A central fountain in a classical style would provide the finishing touch.

If creating a pool from scratch, make it a formal one with raised sides built of concrete facing blocks or bricks. On a more modest level, you could install a wall fountain or a bird bath of formal design, positioned so that it will make a focal point.

Planting

The plants in your Mediterranean garden do not necessarily have to belong to that region — the first rule of successful gardening, as ever, is to grow what will flourish in your micro-climate and soil. Keep most of what you have, but arrange it differently, and punctuate it with unusual and striking plants that are often found in hotter climates.

Divide up a conventional, meandering herbaceous border into neat geometrical shapes; raised beds, created with low walls or railway sleepers, are ideal for this. Plant the beds densely, including as many silver-grey-leaved and spiky plants as you can. Sea holly (*Eryngium*), giant thistle (*Onopordum*) and *Cineraria maritima* will all fill the bill.

For the sub-tropical effect, add a few architectural foliage plants such as century plants (*Agave)*, New Zealand flax (*Phormium tenax*) and yuccas. Semi-hardy palms are also good – look for European fan palm (*Chamaerops humilis*), windmill palm (*Trachycarpus fortunei*) and Washington palm (*Washingtonia filifera*).

Containers

Always have plenty of plants in containers, preferably ones made of terracotta or stone, especially around a paved area. Some of these can be used for architectural plants, to provide a focus of interest just where you want it. This

The spiky leaves of yuccas add an authentically exotic architectural note to a Mediterranean garden. Some species have a basal rosette of spiky leaves; others, such as Spanish dagger (Y. gloriosa) carry them in tufts on unbranched stems (above). These are 'Variegata', with golden margins to their leaves.

French marigolds (Tagetes patula) are excellent container subjects, and will bring a splash of hot colour to a sunny spot (right). Here, the colours are cooled by a variegated hosta and a blue lobelia.

also makes it easy to move tender plants inside during the winter, though beware of using containers so large you cannot shift them when they are full of earth.

Hot flowers

For summer bedding, use the hottest, strongest colours you can find – scarlet, yellow and shocking pink rather than pastels and blues. Nasturtiums, French marigolds, petunias and salvias all come in the right bold colours, but above all make good use of bedding geraniums (pelargoniums). Al-

though they may not flower quite as exuberantly as they do in the hot Mediterranean sun, the new F1 varieties in particular, planted in warm sheltered spots, will put up a wonderful show lasting until the first frosts. Always include plenty of the cascading or ivy-leaved varieties which will tumble abundantly over the edges of containers, just as they do in Italy.

To clothe the walls, use some of the more exotic

Formal hedging can find its place in a Mediterranean garden (top). In this Italian garden, an arch has been cut from a tall hedge to create a bower. This provides both a cool place to sit and a dark area, framed in green, against which to view the sunlit plants.

The lovely flowers of the deciduous trumpet vine (Campsis radicans) appear in late summer (above).

climbers such as passion flower (*Passiflora caerulea*), which is evergreen, with large mauve and white flowers; or trumpet vine (*Campsis*), which is deciduous, with spectacular, orange-red, trumpet-shaped flowers.

High walls inevitably bring shade for part of the day. In these areas use plants with golden or gold-splashed leaves, such as *Elaeagnus*, *Euonymous* and *Hosta fortunei* 'Aureomarginata', to create an illusion of sunlight. A small, golden-leaved conifer is ideal for brightening a dark corner all year round. Similarly, clothe a north-facing wall with the evergreen honeysuckle *Lonicera japonica* 'Aureoreticulata', which has bright green leaves netted with gold.

Suitable trees

A Mediterranean garden is above all sunny, so avoid large trees that cast a lot of shade. An existing one should be

professionally thinned and reduced in height to let in more light. Flowering cherries are very suitable, giving you early spring blossom and remaining fairly compact. *Prunus* 'Amanogawa' is especially good for a tiny garden, as its branches all point upwards, like those of a poplar.

Any small, upright-growing conifer will add the right touch in summer and winter too – but beware the giants. The Italian cypress whose pencil-like outline and deep green, almost black, aromatic foliage is such a feature of the Mediterranean scene is *Cupressus sempervirens* 'Stricta'. It should not grow more than about 4.5m/15ft high.

A feature of larger Mediterranean gardens is a paved area covered by a pergola and sometimes partially enclosed with pillars and low walls or trellis. The disadvantage with these in less sunny climates is that they will probably cast more shade than is desirable for all but a very few days in the year. However, if you erect a pergola in a place that is already shaded you have nothing to lose, and the effect, once the bare wood is clothed with a grape vine, roses or jasmine, is instantly Continental.

Always use planed timber to build such structures in the Mediterranean garden, as rustic poles or their like detract from the formal look.

Furniture

As the Mediterranean garden is usually viewed as an outdoor room, garden furniture is essential. For a Continental look, choose chairs and small tables made in aluminium but using traditional cast-iron designs. An alternative is the painted, slatted, wooden designs reminiscent of French parks. Existing timber garden seats can be painted white.

Picnic tables with integral benches are really a North American invention, but blend in quite well. A true Mediterranean garden more often features an incredibly ancient, knocked together, wooden table, proudly bearing the ring marks and scars of countless *al fresco* meals.

Table umbrellas and window awnings are much used in a genuine Mediterranean garden – although rarely necessary in the British climate, they help to create the right look.

The half-hardy annual Salvia splendens blazes with fiery colour in the late summer and early autumn. The species is a solid red, but some varieties are bi-coloured, while others, such as 'Phoenix Mixed' (right) boast shades of pink and purple.

Paving is an acceptable alternative to gravel, especially when it is of a light-coloured stone (below). Here the Mediterranean ambience is heightened by the style of the house, with its white walls, pantiles, louvred shutters, and wrought iron balcony, as well as a colourful collection of Impatiens spilling out of their containers.

A Bog Garden

By turning a small area of your garden into a bog, you will provide an environment in which both wildlife and a host of fascinating and lovely plants will flourish.

The term 'bog garden' lacks romantic appeal, conjuring up visions of desolate, midge-infested marshes at the edge of civilization, of mud and mess and general unpleasantness. Words like 'fascinating', 'charming' and 'beautiful' do not spring instantly to mind; but they should. Some of the loveliest plants in the world dwell in wetlands.

Most people will have to create a bog; the best conditions rarely occur naturally in gardens. Although the word 'bog' is used loosely for any soggy place, a bog garden **must** have adequate drainage or it will become waterlogged and stagnant. Stagnant water allows a build up of hostile micro-organisms in the soil that will eventually kill off your precious plants.

Why a bog?

A bog garden fills a special role in a well-planned informal garden, bridging the gap between dry land and water features. A formal pond lends itself to the stark contrast between land and water, but informal gardening is more about blurring boundaries, and the gentle movement from one form to another.

A bog is an important addition to a wildlife pond, providing not only a vital micro-environment but also a way in and out of the water for amphibians such as frogs and toads. Birds will use its fringes for collecting tasty morsels and for easy access to the pond for drinking and bathing.

A variety of useful and interesting insects will also live and breed in this miniature marshland, including, with luck, brilliantly colourful dragon and damsel flies.

First and foremost, though, a bog garden is the ideal environment for a host of truly wonderful plants, from the tall and stately to the small and homely. There are glorious foliage plants as well as those with colourful blooms.

Bog gardens are usually seen as an extension to a pond, and this is certainly a practical place for one. The combination of bog and pond closely resembles nature's way of doing things, and the bog helps integrate the pond with the rest of the garden.

This scheme does not suit everyone. Ponds are not a good idea if you have very young children, for instance. You can

Few people associate bogs with lush growth, but a wet, well-drained area can support an intriguing mix of lovely flowering and foliage plants (above). When the bog garden is associated with a pond or, as here, a small stream, there is the added bonus that the flowers and leaves are reflected in the water.

The meadowsweet (Filipendula ulmaria syn. Spiraea ulmaria) has a wonderfully sweet, pervasive scent. It carries its heads of creamy-white flowers high above its divided foliage in the summer. The young leaves of the variety 'Aurea' (left) have golden-green variegations.

Bog gardens are usually found in informal, wildlife gardens, but a bog area can be incorporated into a more formal plan (below). Here, a rectangular bog beside the pool is home to a colourful display of white and blue irises, coral pink astilbes, and the golden blooms and deeply divided foliage of a globeflower (Trollius).

however combine a bog garden with running water features.

A handsome – and totally safe – alternative is to combine your bog garden with a dry stream feature made of attractive rocks and pebbles. A bubble fountain splashing over the pebbles will bring the soothing sound of running water to your garden as it tops up the bog.

A short, shallow water course, with a boggy area incorporated along its banks is another option. A recirculating pump and a sunken tank will make this possible. It is also perfectly possible to make a bog garden without any still or running water feature.

It is a simple matter to incorporate a bog garden into a new pond. Allow extra pond-

Many candelabra primulas – named for the way the whorls of flowers are arranged in tiers up the stems – thrive in damp conditions, and the wide range of varieties on offer add greatly to the bog gardener's palette of colours. Here (left) pink and purple varieties are grouped with the yellow monkey flower (Mimulus luteus).

liner to cover the boggy area. Dig out your pond to the required depth and excavate a hollow, about 30cm/1ft deep, alongside it.

Make a ridge between the pond and the bog area. Without this barrier you will either end up with a larger pond than you planned or your pond water will drain away into the bog. It may be made by piling up rocks and stones or rolled-

up turves. If you use rocks and stones, cover them with turf or an old bit of carpet, so that the jagged edges do not rip your liner. The top of the ridge should be marginally below the water level of the pond so that water occasionally laps over on to the bog.

Extend your pond liner over the ridge into the hollow and puncture it several times at its deepest point. This will allow water to drain out slowly.

Line the hollow with a 5cm/2in layer of pebbles and then

another 5cm/2in layer of coarse peat, peat substitute or chopped, turfy loam. If you have a few turves left over after making a lawn, then use them for the second layer, placing them grass side down.

Top the whole thing off with

soil mixed with liberal amounts of well-rotted manure, leaf mould, peat or peat substitute, and coarse sand.

It does not matter if the level of the finished bog is a little higher than the pond, but do not pile the soil up too high, or

One of the most popular choices for the bog garden is the king cup or marsh marigold (Caltha palustris). A relative of the meadow buttercup, it has similar, though larger, golden flowers in the spring, wonderfully set off by mounds of glossy, dark green, rounded leaves (above).

In most gardens, bogs are associated with ponds, and it makes good practical sense to create both at the same time. Two adjacent hollows are dug out and lined; one is filled with water and the other with suitably prepared soil (left).

Many irises enjoy soggy soil. The beardless Siberian iris (I. sibirica) is one of these, producing early summer flowers in the blue to purple colour range. 'Savoir Faire' (left) is a particularly richly coloured variety.

it will silt up your pond.

Do not surround your entire pond with a marshy margin because you will need access to both the pond and the bog for routine maintenance.

The independent bog

The method for creating a bog garden away from a pond is very similar. An advantage is that you can use polythene, cheaper than butyl or PVC, as a liner. This material is not suitable for ponds, as it degrades when exposed to light.

With no lapping water to keep the site damp, you must be generous with the turves in your second layer, as this will help to hold water. The soil of your top layer must be a rich mixture of moisture-retaining material, so do not be tempted to skimp on this.

A careful choice of site helps here. If it is near to trees, their roots will rob the bog garden of moisture. Partial shade will help a lot, but you must be careful to select plants to tolerate these conditions.

A much simpler, if slightly less reliable method is to fill your punctured liner with ordinary garden soil and to flood it from time to time with a hose to keep it moist.

Going shopping

Water garden centres will have a wide range of bog garden plants, but any garden centre will be able to provide you with a selection of common garden plants that prefer boggy conditions.

Astilbes, for instance, enjoy moist soils, and will provide plume-like summer flower heads in shades of pink from a

When the bog garden area is in light or partial shade, foliage plants such as hostas and ferns often put on the best display (below).

pale, sugary hue to a deep, rich one and a selection of reds from burgundy to raspberry. There are several white varieties, too. Most astilbes enjoy partial shade.

Day lilies (*Hemerocallis* spp.) come in a wide palette of warm colours and produce a succession of spectacular flowers through the summer, each exotic bloom lasting just a day. They are often fragrant.

For foliage interest in a bog garden, it is hard to beat the moisture-loving hostas, whose bold, often variegated leaves look at their best when reflected in a pool.

Many plants of the *Primula* genus enjoy damp conditions. The vigorous Himalayan cowslip (*P. florindae*) produces tall sprays of fragrant yellow flowers similar to the wild cowslip, while the various candelabra primulas have primrose-like flowers. These in-

Primula japonica (right), like the other candelabra primulas, has an upright growth habit; its flower stems grow up to 60cm/2ft tall above the rosettes of flat leaves typical of primulas. There is an excellent white variety, 'Postford White' (seen in the photograph on p.942) but most are red or reddish-pink.

The bogbean (Menyanthes trifoliata) is a marginal plant that likes its roots in water. However, when planted at the edge of the pond it often spreads into the boggy area round about, and vice versa. It is primarily grown for its pinkish white flowers, which have a distinctive fringe of white hairs (below).

THE DRAINAGE TEST

Dig a hole about 60cm/2ft deep and wait for rain. Check the hole regularly to see what happens.

If there is no water left in the hole a few days afterwards, you will have to use a liner to inhibit drainage, but if there is just a little water at the bottom of the hole, you are in luck. There is no need for a liner; just dig a hole and fill it with the usual three layers of material.

Sometimes you will find water has seeped into your test hole from the surrounding area. This means the spot is likely to get too waterlogged, and drainage must be improved before you create a bog garden.

GARDEN NOTES

A form of campion, ragged Robin (Lychnis flos-cuculi) is a fairly common wild plant in marshy areas and meadows in Britain. A perennial, it earns its place in the bog garden with its distinctive, pinkish flowers, with thin 'ragged' petals flaring out from tubular calyces (right).

Many bog garden plants grow naturally in the wet, well-drained soil to be found on the banks of streams and, if you have room, the recreation of such an environment in the garden can make a stunning feature (below). Here, the natural look is enhanced not only by the wild jumble of planting but also by the judicious use of such features as wooden retainers and rounded stones and pebbles.

clude the rosy-purple *P. bee-siana* and the red *P. japonica*. The latter has a white variety, 'Postford White', with an alluring golden eye.

Several members of the large iris family thrive in bogs, adding height and distinction to the planting scheme, their upright, spiky leaves making a fine contrast with the foliage of ferns and hostas.

Wild wetlands

You can add to the natural look of an informal scheme by planting any of a host of wild or naturalized plants that suit

damp and boggy conditions.

Wild angelica (*Angelica sylvestris*), for instance, is a tall, white umbellifer that flowers in late summer. The garden form, *A. archangelica*, has fresh green flowers and also prefers moist soils.

Bogbean (*Menyanthes trifoliata*) has pinkish flowers fringed with long white hairs. It likes very boggy ground, as does the marsh marigold (*Caltha palustris*), with its gloriously rich yellow flowers.

Ragged Robin (*Lychnis flos-cuculi*) has bright pink, ragged petals and makes a gorgeous addition to your bog garden, as does the monkey flower (*Mimulus luteus*), with its bright yellow flowers speckled with red and brown.

Meadowsweet (*Filipendula ulmaria*) will bring a sweet scent and frothy, creamy flowers to your scheme, while the marsh cinquefoil (*Potentilla palustris*) is valued for its deep red to purple, star-shaped flowers and its fondness for acid soils.

The Fragrant Garden

Delicious scents carried on warm summer breezes cast an intoxicating spell. Plant a selection of fragrant flowers for your very own perfumed garden.

There is a feeling of tranquility and peace in the scented garden, a sense of timelessness. Sadly, however, fragrance is often the last thing to be considered when designing a garden, if it is considered at all.

A garden planted for fragrance is an unusual creation, but a delightful one. Different scents can be used to enhance and emphasize the overall character or theme of the garden. Colour may still be the most important design consideration, but by selecting scented plants that fit the chosen colour scheme wherever possible, you can add a whole new dimension to the garden experience.

In describing scents, we tend to compare them to well-

The sights and scents of summer are summed up by everyone's favourite flower – the rose. Its honeyed perfume is attractive to bees and butterflies as well as to the gardener.

known, easily recognizable fragrances such as rose, violet, honey, spice, lemon or mint. Smells can also be described as being sweet, aromatic, rich, heavy or pungent.

Many and varied scents

To appreciate fully the subtleties of fragrance, take the time to explore several gardens and familiarize yourself with the rich and varied world of plant scents. Experience the fragrances not only of flowers and leaves but stems, roots, bark, seeds and resins. Revisit gardens in the evening, as many scents are only apparent at this time of day.

You will find the rich and intoxicating fragrance of some plants wafting across the garden. Other plants are more modest about their perfumes, requiring you to plunge your nose into their petals or pinch their leaves before they surrender their delicious smells.

You will also discover that the most fragrant flowers tend to be in white or pastel shades, not dazzling colours; their scent attracts bees and butterflies. Happily, pale flowers

harmonize well with less aromatic, brilliantly coloured blooms, allowing you to mix and match with different colour schemes. You can then create a garden design that is both visually pleasing and delightfully fragrant.

There are many different ways of creating your own scented haven or adding delightful pockets of fragrance to an established garden.

Scents can be confined to certain areas of your garden to create zones of fragrances and these can be separated by scentless flowers, so distinctive smells do not mingle. Each zone may evoke a separate mood or character.

Scents can also be used to

Wander down this camomile path (above) and each step you take will crush these sturdy little plants, releasing their peppery aroma into the air. Here it will mingle with the scents of the lavender and roses in the carefully planned fragrant borders. These are all old-fashioned fragrances that evoke the atmosphere of a typical country cottage garden.

reflect a particular colour theme. For instance, lemon scents are just right in a predominantly yellow garden, while rich, spicy aromas suit a garden full of deep purples, reds and golds.

Scented plants are particularly effective when situated beside a garden path or scattered around the edge of a lawn. On the other hand, you may decide to devote a small area of garden to scent.

Scented species can also be featured individually, so that a particular fragrance can be savoured in isolation. Rose gardens and herb gardens are often designed as separate areas for this reason.

Use the plan, below, as a guideline when planning a scented garden of your own. The area you allocate can be as large or as small as you like. An essential element, however, is a place to sit down and enjoy the fragrance.

The seat can be a permanent

A SCENTED GARDEN

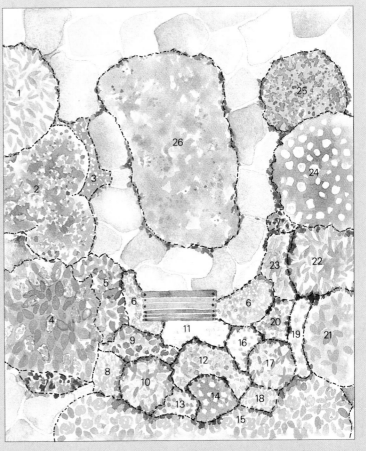

The plan is for an area of garden 4.5 × 5.5m/15 × 18ft, but can easily be scaled up or down. The sizes and colours of plants are carefully varied, but this can also be changed.

1. summersweet (clethra)
2. three Ghent hybrid azaleas
3. sweet woodruff
4. lilac
5. tobacco plants
6. sweet alyssum
7. violets
8. chrysanthemums
9. phlox
10. peonies
11. artemesia
12. pinks
13. tree lupins
14. regal lilies
15. four shrub roses
16. mignonette
17. peonies
18. chrysanthemums
19. day lilies
20. pinks
21. fragrant viburnum
22. summersweet (clethra)
23. snapdragons
24. mock orange
25. daphne
26. a thyme lawn

The clove pink is so named because it smells of cloves. This named variety, Dianthus carophyllus 'Cherry Ripe' (right) is guaranteed to add not only fragrance but a splash of bright colour to your beds and borders. Once cut, it lasts well in water, so use it in flower arrangements where its scent can be enjoyed indoors as well as out.

Because of its heady, orange-blossom fragrance, philadelphus (above) is commonly known as mock orange. The pretty white flowers of this hardy deciduous shrub appear in clusters in early summer.

fixture, such as a bench, or you may prefer a paved area large enough to arrange deckchairs or even a garden table and chairs for al fresco meals.

Every element in the plan can be varied to suit your own garden. Replace the thyme lawn with camomile, for example, surround the seat not with low-growing sweet alyssum but bushes of lavender and add spring-flowering bulbs such as snowdrops and grape hyacinths.

Even the overall shape can be changed to a more formal layout with straight edges, and perhaps a brick path, or gravel, instead of flagstones.

Plant placement is a very important consideration. Plants that release their fragrances easily, such as roses, honeysuckle and jasmine can be located some distance from pathways and seating areas so their lovely scents are wafted on gentle breezes.

Most scented plants are not so richly perfumed, however, and need to be placed within easy reach. One of the most important considerations in planning your scented garden is ensuring that the plants are readily accessible.

Sit and savour

Plants with delicately scented flowers and leaves ideally should be placed near paths or seating areas where they can be touched or squeezed to release their fragrance. Plants

When the sweet smells of summer have started to fade, the citrus scent of lemon verbena is waiting to be savoured. Grow it in a tub (left) to be located wherever it can be most appreciated.

Similarly, night-scented stock (right) is best grown near a patio or terrace where you can sit on summer evenings and enjoy its strong scent.

Hollygrape (far right) is an evergreen shrub whose showy yellow flowers will enrich a winter garden with their sweet scent.

such as camomile, thyme or penny royal can be grown between paving stones or in a path. Their lovely aromas are released as you step on them.

Elevating the senses

Fragrant flowers are often the main attraction in gardens designed for the blind or partially sighted. Often, these plants are grown in raised beds so their fragrances can be enjoyed at nose level. Handling and touching the plants is encouraged, to release smells and to help develop an appreciation for differences in shapes and textures.

You can use this idea in your own garden. Try growing fragrant plants in raised beds, hanging baskets, containers and window boxes. Placed near doors and windows, their wonderful scents can be enjoyed both inside and out. It is a lovely way of enriching the lives of people who may have to spend a lot of time indoors.

Preserving the perfume

The fragrant mixtures of dried flowers known as pot pourri are commercially available, but when you have a garden full of scented plants it is more rewarding to make your own,

SCENTED PLANT SELECTION

Make your own selection of perfumed plants from the following list, noting scent and flowering times:

Winter-flowering

wintersweet (*Chimonanthus praecox*)	violet
crocus (*Crocus chrysanthus*)	delicate
mezereon (*Daphne mezereum*)	violet
witch hazel (*Hamamelis mollis*)	sweet/strong
hollygrape (*Mahonia lomariifolia*)	sweet
viburnum (*Viburnum farreri*)	rich

Spring-flowering

lily-of-the-valley (*Convallaria majalis*)	rich
snowdrops (*Galanthus* species)	honey
iris (*Iris reticulata*)	violet
snowflake (*Leucojum vernum*)	violet
magnolia (*Magnolia* species)	sweet
grape hyacinth (*Muscari armeniacum*)	rich
osmanthus (*Osmanthus delavayi*)	sweet
rhododendrons and azaleas (*Rhododendron* species)	sweet

Summer-flowering

snapdragons (*Antirrhinum majus*)	sweet
pot marigold (*Calendula officinalis*)	pungent
hawthorn (*Crataegus species*)	sweet
clematis (*Clematis montana* and hybrids)	sweet/strong
pinks/carnations (*Dianthus* species)	sweet
gilia (*Gilia tricolor*)	chocolate
day lilies (*Hemerocallis* species)	sweet
lavender (*Lavandula* species)	lavender
beebalm (*Monarda didyma*)	sweet
regal lily (*Lilium regale*)	rich
phlox (*Phlox paniculata*)	sweet
mock orange (*Philadelphus coronarius*)	orange
salvia (*Salvia* species)	aromatic
lilac (*Syringa* species)	rich

Autumn-flowering

yarrow (*Achillea filipendulina*)	pungent (leaves)
southernwood (*Artemisia abrotanum*)	aromatic (leaves)
chrysanthemum (*Chrysanthemum* species)	aromatic (leaves)
crocus (*Crocus sativus*)	sweet
elaeagnus (*Elaeagnus pungens*)	sweet
jasmine (*Jasminum officinale*)	jasmine
lemon verbena (*Lippia citriodora*)	lemon
osmanthus (*Osmanthus heterophyllis*)	sweet
honeysuckle (*Lonicera japonica* 'Aureoreticulata')	sweet

Surround yourself with lavender by planting it round a garden bench (above), or grow it in generous clumps alongside a path (right). Both leaves and flowers have a strong, very characteristic perfume. Harvest the flowers to scent your house or dry them to make pot pourri.

If you grow tobacco plants in a raised bed, the aroma can be appreciated at 'nose' level. Colourful, easy to grow and shade-tolerant, they flower all summer long. The tube-shaped, starry flowers open up in the evening to release their sweet fragrance.

In this bed (left) a clump of trailing ivy, Hedera helix 'Glacier' softens the edge of the bricks and provides a soft contrast to the bright red flowers.

FLOWER ARRANGING

The following fragrant flowers last well when cut:
Peruvian lilies
- pot marigold
- wallflower
- chrysanthemums
- hyacinths
- bearded iris
- sweet peas
- regal lily
- paeony
- roses

and preserve the scents of summer all year long.

A basic mixture might include rose petals, lavender flowers, lemon verbena leaves, camomile flowers, herbs and scented geranium leaves.

The flowers should ideally be picked after a long dry spell, although not when the weather has been so dry that the plants are wilting from lack of water. However, especially later in the year, you may find that you have to make a choice between waiting for the moment when the flowers reach perfection and beating the first frosts and gales which could very easily ruin a whole year's work.

Harvest on a dry day. Wait until the dew has evaporated, but try not to pick when it is too hot as the flowers may be wilting or in the evening when they may be damp. Shake the stems to dislodge any insects hiding unseen among the petals. Spread the petals and leaves to dry in single layers on sheets of absorbent paper and place in a warm, dry place, out of direct sunlight. When dry, mix them together. Add freshly ground spices, drops of perfumed oil or essences, or pieces of dried lemon, lime or orange peel, if you wish. Put the finished product in bowls and scatter them round your home to bring a fresh smell of summer all year round or give them to friends and relatives as an ideal gift. When the scent starts to fade, revitalize it with a few drops of the appropriate perfumed oil or essence.

An Oriental Garden

Oriental gardens, though far removed from their Western equivalents, are full of ideas for creating beautiful, serene effects in a limited space.

The oriental gardener creates effects by playing on the textures and subtle shadings of foliage (above). Natural materials such as stones and pebbles are chosen to enhance the natural effect and for their symbolic value; here, a winding stone and pebble path represents a stream.

The sublime tranquillity of the oriental garden is no accident. The extraordinary peacefulness that pervades every leaf and stone, enhanced by subtle colour, uncluttered plantings and a wonderful sense of space, is generated by using some simple but highly-disciplined design principles.

It is the achievement of generations of religious and philosophical thought far removed from Western ideas, but with a similar aim. Both East and West seek restful surroundings as a retreat from the bustle of daily life, especially that of a busy, urban environment. We share a love of nature's beauty, recreating it in our gardens to restore the spirit and give enjoyment to ourselves and our friends.

But, while Western gardens are often an abundance of crammed colour celebrating nature's variety, the Chinese or Japanese gardener attempts to recreate the magnificence of the natural landscape with the simplicity of an oriental painting.

In the garden, every detail – the line of a single branch, the moss on a stone, the glint of water through leaves – symbolizes a different aspect of the natural world. Each element is carefully chosen according to a strict code laid down over generations. The vastness and variety of the natural landscape can be suggested in a manner as simple as the Japanese dry gardens of rock and sand, and in the smallest of spaces, down to a perfect miniature garden in a bowl.

Over the threshold

In the oriental world, the sanctity of the home is paramount. The house and garden are treated as one, linked by a covered veranda with no balustrade which opens the living-rooms to the garden and allows it to be viewed from a slightly elevated position.

The Chinese philosophy of *yin-yang* (known as *in-yo* in Japan) sees the world as the expression of harmony between contrasts; between light, strength and masculinity on the one hand, and twilight, delicacy and femininity on the other. So in the garden, it is essential to retain a balance between such contrasting ele-

93

Floral colour is used for an accent in oriental gardens. Water hawthorn (Eichhornia crassipes, right) adds colour to pools with its spikes of lilac or blue summer flowers. A floating plant, it increases rapidly and can prove invasive, though it is generally checked by frost.

RECOMMENDED PLANTS

When choosing plants for an oriental-style garden, consider their contribution to subtle contrasts of texture, building light and shade, balancing vertical and horizontal lines and, above all, retaining an uncluttered elegance.

Trees are often placed singly to make the most of their individual characteristics. Varieties of Japanese maple (*Acer palmatum*) are chosen for beauty of form and leaf and autumn colour, including the delicate texture of 'Dissectum'. Flowering cherry (*Prunus*) provides spring blossom and autumn colour. *P. sargentii* is slow-growing, but will, after many years, reach some 8m/25ft – 'Accolade' is a smaller hybrid. *P.* 'Shimidsu Sakura' is widely-branching, reaching about 3m/10ft. Pines and conifers are chosen for evergreen foliage. The mountain pine (*Pinus mugo*), growing to about 2m/6ft, has an interesting spreading habit with a rather tangled appearance, evocative of the natural landscape.

Foliage Bamboos may be too vigorous for small gardens, but try *Pleioblastus viridistriatus* (syn. *Arundinaria viridistriata*), with its 1-1.5m/3-5ft purple stems and yellow-striped leaves. Blue fescue (*Festuca glauca*) and golden *Hakonechloa macra* 'Aureola' are excellent grasses. For ferns, try *Adiantum pedatum* (the Northern maidenhair fern) and *A. venustum*, both with beautifully delicate fronds – these prefer neutral to acid soil. Hostas provide good sculptural foliage, while box (*Buxus sempervirens*) can be clipped into neat boulder-like domes. For authentic effects, allow mosses and lichens some freedom. Otherwise, substitute Mind-your-own-business (*Soleirolia soleirolii* syn. *Helxine soleirolii*), or carpeting alpines such as *Saxifraga moschata* 'Cloth of Gold', which will bring light, golden touches to shadier spots.

Flowering plants such as azalea, rhododendron, camellia, iris, peony, chrysanthemum and Japanese quince (*Chaenomeles speciosa*) are used selectively.

Water plants The grass-like leaves of *Typha minima* contrast well with water lilies (*Nymphaea*) and the invasive, but frost tender water hyacinth (*Eichhornia crassipes*).

*The simple principles of oriental garden design can be scaled down and adapted to some unusual sites (left). Here, a corner of a city rooftop has been screened off and a young, container-grown Japanese larch (*Larix kaempferi*) has been 'underplanted' with a variegated ivy and tubs containing Fatsia japonica and an azalea. Large, water-smoothed stones complete the picture. This pleasing arrangement depends on the fast-growing larch being pruned regularly; left to its own devices it matures into a very tall tree.*

ments as light and shade, angular and curved contours, and stone and water.

Since the natural landscape has no rigid boundaries, different devices are used to obscure the limits of the garden and increase the sense of space.

Dense plantings, often with conifers, mask the fence, and are glimpsed through the branches of trees with more open habits and lighter foliage, such as flowering cherries, which are planted nearer the house. Elements from neighbouring gardens become part of the picture, continuing the landscape beyond the fence, while pathways meander through the garden, twisting away out of sight into an imaginary distance.

Planned informality
The regularity and symmetry of Western formal gardens are disliked in the East. The oriental gardener admires instead the irregular in all its variety, symbolizing the uncertainty of nature. Great delight is taken in the weathered surface of a stone, the asymmetrical arrangement of a few plants or boulders, and in the positioning of a tree so that a branch partially hides some other feature of the garden.

Natural harmony
Above all, the gardener must work in harmony with nature itself. Even fences, which enclose the entire garden for privacy, must be of natural materials – usually bamboo or wood. Where a solid screen is not necessary, they are often of a slightly open pattern, allowing glimpses of greenery beyond the garden.

Stone and water are essential elements, taken direct from the natural landscape. The gardener will search for days for the right stones, delighting most in those from streams or the seashore which reflect the actions of nature in their worn surfaces, and perhaps a partial clothing of moss. Stones are admired for their surface texture and colouring, which change with the rain or sun, and are used for paths, for the edges of ponds or beds or simply for their own sake. Shrubs, ferns and grasses enhance by contrast the character of the stone, emphasizing its strength and mass.

Water may be represented symbolically in stone or sand, or feature in a pond, waterfall,

Varieties of Japanese maple (Acer palmatum 'Dissectum') are ideal for a Japanese-style garden; the purple, divided leaves of 'Atropupuream' (left) turn red in autumn.

It can take decades, even centuries, to grow miniature trees – bonsai – in a bowl, and their price reflects this, but they are a true ornament to a garden (above).

MINIATURE GARDENS

The ability to express the greatest landscape in the smallest space reaches its peak in the miniature landscapes created within the confines of a single bowl.

These started out as arrangements of sand, pebbles and small rocks, with a little greenery. Different stones represented specific elements of the natural landscape; mountains, seashores, even lakes.

Then gardeners discovered the art of growing miniature trees by cutting back and binding the roots of seedlings. These *bonsai* (grown in a bowl) have all the features of a tree growing in the great outdoors, but on the tiniest scale, and have become the most highly-prized feature of the Japanese miniature garden.

Bonsai are classified according to the shape into which they have been painstakingly trained, perhaps over hundreds of years. Those with upright, straight trunks suggest a forest setting, while sloping trunks are reminiscent of windswept cliffs, and dwarf pines with cascading branches speak of waterfalls.

The beauty of *bonsai* and miniature gardens is their size, allowing them to be moved wherever their picture of nature is needed to restore the spirit, perhaps in the living-room or inside the front door as a welcoming gesture to visitors.

som, green summer foliage, autumnal colour and tracery of naked branches in winter.

In larger gardens, different trees may represent each season, with the Japanese maple (*Acer palmatum*) ablaze in autumn, and an ornamental crab apple (*Malus*) bearing its decorative fruit into winter.

The Japanese and Chinese place much less emphasis on colour than the West; plants are chosen more for the subtle tones and harmonies they add than for their brilliance. Foliage, therefore, is the main interest, with plants chosen for their leaf shape and texture. Moss is highly-prized, and bamboo, ferns and grasses are all prominent features.

Flowers add just a few accents of colour. Chrysanthemums have become as much an emblem of the Orient as the rose is of England, and, together with the azalea, iris, peony and lily, are chosen for their traditional symbolic associations with ideas of long life, blessedness, peace and everlasting happiness.

Basins and lanterns

Ornament is not essential to the oriental garden. Too much of it can destroy the tranquil sense of space, by overcrowding and distracting the eye from the subtleties of the 'natural' landscape. The water ba-

Ferns, with their subtle colours and unusual textures, can always find a place in an oriental garden. The delicate, tumbling fronds of Adiantum venustum *(right) will soon cover a semi-shady bank.*

In the oriental garden, gravel is used in many ways. Often, it is smoothed and rolled to represent water (left). Here, a path of large flat stepping stones enhances this effect. It also performs the function of a lawn, providing a base against which the delicate shapes and textures of other plants can be appreciated. It has two advantages over grass in this respect; it changes colour to reflect the weather and needs no mowing!

Coarser gravels give a different textural effect (right below), enhanced by contrast with the smoothness of water-rounded stones and pebbles, and make a fitting backdrop for sturdy, low-growing plants such as dwarf conifers.

Larger pebbles – though perhaps too hard on the feet to cover any large area – can make a delightful contrast to foliage plants with bold, undivided leaves, such as hostas (below).

even a basin. Trickling water brings life to the garden in its movement and musical sound, while the flat surface of a pond or basin provides scope for beautiful reflections. Whatever form it takes, a water feature must look as natural as possible, with ferns and aquatic plants mingling with the stones around the edge.

Seasonal cycles

Every aspect of the natural world is suggested in the oriental garden. The changing seasons may be represented in a flowering cherry (*Prunus*), with its delightful spring blos-

DRY GARDENS

The dry gardens of Japan are the ultimate expression of refined simplicity. In the temples of Zen Buddhism, these stark landscapes of rock and sand provided the perfect setting for undistracted meditation. For us they are an excellent source of decorative ideas for small, tranquil spots, and are especially useful in the context of a maintenance-free garden.

In the dry garden, water is suggested by a dry stream bed created from water-worn stones, or in expanses of sand from which rise boulders and rocks representing legendary islands symbolizing long life or joy eternal. Each weathered stone is selected with the greatest care and placed singly or with others in 'natural' asymmetrical groups. An illusion of greater depth is established by placing larger rocks in the foreground.

Often, moss is the only greenery, but small, carefully trimmed bushes such as box are sometimes used instead of boulders. There is no reason why a western equivalent should not be enlivened with just a handful of plants such as ferns, grasses and hostas, their foliage softening the mass of a boulder and contrasting well with the stark background.

The expanse of sand in temple gardens is meticuously raked into traditional patterns. Parallel lines represent waves, while ellipses and circles round stones are like water breaking on the rocks of an island.

These patterns need continuous attention to counter the disturbance of wind and rain, making them impractical for domestic gardens, unless on a very small scale. However, even a base of unraked gravel or pebbles offers lovely changes of texture and hue with sun and rain.

sin with its bamboo scoop and the stone lantern are, however, permanent features, introduced originally for religious purposes: the basin for cleansing the body and spirit; the lantern to represent the light of knowledge.

The water basin is usually of weathered stone but may be of another natural material – perhaps part of a fallen tree trunk, hollowed out. It is often raised on a flattened stone and enhanced by a very simple arrangement of rock and green foliage plants or moss. Again, the water may be represented by sand or fine gravel.

The idea of the lantern is not to rid the garden of the darkness but to enrich its mystery. It is most effective when placed to one side, perhaps in a shady spot against the foliage of trees and shrubs, whence it will cast intriguing, ever-changing shadows.

Wild Flowers in the Garden

Do your bit for nature and the environment by making room in your garden for some of our increasingly rare native species.

This carefuly contrived wild garden looks completely natural. Native plants like white and mauve dame's violets, blue cornflowers and bright red poppies are grown in bold patches, while yellow Welsh poppies and spikes of mullein have self-seeded. Heartsease grows in drifts, and daisies dot the grass. Once established, a garden like this thrives on a minimum of attention.

Imagine a summer's day in a garden of wild flowers, where all the colours blend into a pastel haze and the air is filled with the perfume of nectar and the humming of bees. If this is your picture of what a wild flower garden should be, then you will be pleased to know that making your dream come true is easier than you think. If, on the other hand, you imagine an invasion of weeds and a tangle of un-

wanted plants, then it is worth thinking again.

Wild flowers are simply plants that, under natural conditions, would grow in the wild: these plants are our native species and they are all perfectly suited to the weather and soils of this country. Many of our traditional garden plants are descended from these native wild flowers. Cottage gardeners long ago would have grown only wild

flowers because these were the only plants available. It was not until breeders began to select particular colours and shapes they liked, crossing native species with plants imported from abroad, that the cultivated garden plant was born. Over the years, more exotic species were introduced and some of our common wild flowers were forgotten.

Wild flowers are now back in fashion. This is partly because

This yellow and white colour scheme (left) has tiny daffodils (Narcissus), as well as the more common larger ones, with ox-eye daisies and tall buttercups growing among green ferns and leaves. The patch of pink campion at the back adds a contrasting note.

The nodding sky-blue harebell (Campanula rotundifolia) (below) must be one of the prettiest small wild flowers, and is perfect for a wild flower garden. Harebells will enjoy a sheltered spot in the rockery, and are ideal for wild meadow areas.

people are aware that too many plants are being threatened with extinction as their natural habitats are destroyed by agriculture and building developments. Gardens are one of the few safe havens for wild flowers, and by introducing even a few plants to your garden you will be helping to safeguard their future.

Pretty, easy plants

Conservation is not the only reason for growing wild flowers. Cowslips, daisies, columbine and primroses are some of the prettiest flowers to be found anywhere and you do not need any special skills to grow them. On the whole, native flowers are better for wildlife too, attracting a wide range of insects and birds. Last but not least, wild flowers do not need to be fussed over with intensive watering and feeding. They will grow strong and healthy in even the smallest garden, as long you choose the right plants for your soil and situation. You may even find that they grow better in the garden than in the wild places around your home.

The first step towards establishing wild flowers is to take a good look at your garden and see what is growing there. Look closely and you will see flowers that were not planted, but just 'turned up': daisies, clover and dandelions grow in the lawn, thistles and bindweed in the flower beds. Once you get to know and recognize these wild flowers, you can decide which you like and which you do not. It is up to you to decide which are your 'weeds' and which are flowers.

Good management

A wild flower garden, like a conventional one, needs management if you are to grow the plants you want, rather than the ones that just happen to grow. There is a myth that wild flower gardens have to be untidy. The truth is, you can grow wild flowers, just like any other garden flowers, in neat, straight rows if you want to, but to create a more natural feel they are best grouped together in patches, giving a pretty, cottage garden effect. If there is room it is also worth allowing nettles, brambles and

TOP FIVE WILD FLOWERS FOR GARDENS

Bluebell *(Hyacinthoides non-scripta)*
The nodding heads of bluebells used to be common in woods and hedgerows but they are becoming less common now. They prefer a lightly shaded position; under a hedge or decidous tree is ideal.

TYPE: Perennial, bulb
COLOUR: Blue
PLANTING TIME: Autumn
FLOWERING TIME: Spring to early summer
HEIGHT: 30-40cm/12-16in
SOIL: Any

Common poppy *(Papaver rhoeas)*
One of the best-known annual wild flowers, the poppy used to be found in cornfields but is now more likely to be seen on disturbed earth on roadside and motorway verges. It can be grown in a sunny border or as part of a wildflower meadow.

TYPE: Annual, seed
COLOUR: Red
SOWING TIME: Spring
FLOWERING TIME: Early to late summer
HEIGHT: 40-60cm/16-24in
SOIL: Any, particularly on poor, stony soils

Cornflower *(Centaurea cyanus)*
Once a widespread 'weed' in cornfields, it makes a pretty border flower for cutting. It prefers a sunny position, where it will attract bees and several different species of butterfly.

TYPE: Annual, seed
COLOUR: Bright blue
SOWING TIME: Spring
FLOWERING TIME: Summer
HEIGHT: 60-90cm/24-36in
SOIL: Any, except chalk

Foxglove *(Digitalis purpurea)*
A native of woodlands, the foxglove thrives in a damp, partially shaded spot. This stately plant looks good grown under tall trees or to give height at the back of the border.

TYPE: Biennial, seed or young plant
COLOUR: Purple
PLANTING TIME: Autumn for flowers the following year
FLOWERING TIME: Summer
HEIGHT: 120cm/48in
SOIL: Acid, moist

Primrose *(Primula vulgaris)*
The primrose has suffered greatly in the wild from being overpicked, but makes an excellent garden plant. It prefers a moist, partially shaded spot under trees or hedges.

TYPE: Perennial, seed or young plant
COLOUR: Yellow
PLANTING TIME: Early spring
FLOWERING TIME: Spring
HEIGHT: 20cm/8in
SOIL: Moist

other undesirable plants to grow in a tiny patch out of sight. Although they are not particularly attractive to us, butterflies and other wildlife love them. A space behind a shed or garage is ideal.

If you are lucky enough to have taken over a new house with a completely bare plot, you can plan the whole garden for wild flowers. Most people, however, decide to introduce them gradually, perhaps making a single wild flower bed or turning the lawn into a meadow. If you have some trees and shrubs then you might want to create a mini-woodland, with carpets of bluebells and shade-loving plants. Even a small pond can have some wild plants in and around it, or better still you might create a marshy area nearby to grow damp-loving plants like purple loosestrife and marsh marigold. As well as increasing the range of plants you can grow, a marshland makes a great home for frogs and toads.

Making a selection

Whatever size your garden, even if you are gardening on a balcony or patio, there are wild flowers to suit you. The main thing to remember is that you do not have to give the whole garden over to wild flowers straight away (although once you get 'hooked' it's easy to get carried away!). Pick and choose the plants and the habitats that suit your circumstances.

First look at the garden to assess the 'habitats' you already have. A large tree is a good starting point, as you can plant a selection of shade-loving bulbs like snowdrops and bluebells around the base.

Bluebells are a woodland plant and are at home in the dappled shade of trees and larger shrubs (left). If you can give them enough space and the right growing conditions, they will spread themselves happily. Bluebell seeds are available, and are usually sold as Hyacinthoides non-scripta, but are also sometimes known as Endymion non-scriptus.

To some people, the red dead nettles growing among these primulas in a cool but sunny border (right) are weeds. But a weed is only a plant growing in the wrong place, and if you like a native plant it deserves a place in your flower garden. You may sometimes find you need to thin these plants quite ruthlessly though, as they can be rampant growers if they are made welcome.

You could also put in groups of primroses and sweet violets followed by red campion for the summer. A wet spot or the margins of a pond can be turned into a mini-wetland. This is the place to grow moisture-loving plants like the delicate cuckoo flower, yellow flag iris, meadowsweet and ragged robin. Even the pond itself can have native plants, and planting some curled pondweed or spiked water milfoil which grow under water will help to keep the water clean and clear.

Other wild flowers prefer a

P ROJECT COLLECT YOUR OWN SEEDS

Once you have started growing a few wild flowers in the garden, it is easy and economical to collect your own seed to grow into more plants or to pass on to other gardening friends.

● Wait until the seed pods are ripe. This will vary from plant to plant but is usually when the pods have turned from green to brown.

● Snip off the seed pods with scissors or small secateurs and place them inside a paper bag. Shake the bag until all the seed has been released.

● Lay the contents of the bag on a tray and pick out any bits of stem or plant debris. Leave the seed to dry in the sun or in a warm spot indoors. Store the dry seed in paper envelopes or in clean, sealed jars – spice jars are ideal.

Remember to collect only one type of seed at a time and mark the envelopes and jars clearly to avoid mixing up different species.

No specialist equipment is required for you to begin collecting seeds. Dried seed can be kept in airtight storage jars or an envelope until it is needed. Jars should be clearly labelled (right) as many smaller seeds look very much alike.

sunny spot and a soil that has been turned over and are best grown in a separate flower bed. Poppies, cornflowers, corncockles and corn marigolds are annuals which flower for only one year. Choose a sunny position in the garden and they will provide you with beautiful cut flowers all summer long. It is also easy to add perennial wild flowers to an existing herbaceous border. Plants like meadow cranes-bill, harebell and musk mallow will flower year after year and bring a host of bees and butterflies to your cottage garden border.

Meadow flowers

You might want to try making a wild flower meadow instead of a smooth lawn. If you have an area of bare earth, you can sow a new flowering lawn with meadow mixture. These seed mixtures, available from some garden centres or by mail order from specialist seedsmen, have the right balance of grasses and low-growing wild flowers and are best sown in the autumn. If you already have an established lawn, let it grow then weed out some of the undesirables such as thistles and dock and put cowslips, ox-eye daisies and lady's bedstraw in their place.

Maintaining a wild flower lawn is quite straightforward; continue to mow it, but to a

height of 5-7cm/2-3in rather than the usual 2.5cm/1in. The only exception is from late spring to mid-summer, the main flowering period, when you need to leave the grass uncut to allow the flowers to produce and spread their seeds.

Wild flowers are perfect for a cottage garden border (above), and they can all be grown from seed. Little pockets of soil in wall crevices will encourage ferns and other plants to make a home there.

DON'T FORGET!

IN THE EYES OF THE LAW

Under the Wildlife and Countryside Act 1981 (UK) it is against the law to dig up or disturb any plant in the wild without the landowner's permission. In addition, there are nearly 100 species which cannot be disturbed *at all* because they are so rare. There is really no need to take plants from the wild as garden centres, nurseries and seedsmen now sell bulbs, plants and packets of seed.

Plants naturally grow best in their favourite type of habitat. A boggy area (above) provides the perfect setting for damp-garden plants. If you have a pond, growing plants in the water will help to keep the water clear, as well as adding to the 'wild' look. There is a wide range of moisture-loving plants available in special garden centres. This sort of garden can be made on a very small scale in a damp, shady corner.

Musk mallow, (Malva moschata), (left) is a very colourful wild plant that needs a sunny spot. It can be naturalized in grass.

Growing wild flowers from seed can be time consuming but is not difficult. Annual seeds such as poppies and cornflowers can be sown straight out in the garden in the spring and will flower the same summer.

A wild flower garden is not a neglected garden and will need some regular maintenance, particularly if it is not to become overgrown. Watering is not usually necessary, except for plants grown in containers which dry out quickly in the summer. Likewise, feeding is unnecessary and most wild species prefer no added fertilizer.

The most important task is to deadhead some of the more invasive plants. Simply cut off the heads after they have flowered to stop the seeds being

PRESSING WILD FLOWERS

BRIGHT IDEAS

To prolong the beauty of your wild flowers, you can dry and press them to make pictures or greetings cards. The delicate colours and shapes can be perfectly preserved either as whole flowers or as individual petals. The secret of successful pressing is to cut the flowers on a dry day and to press them immediately, before the colours begin to fade.

You can buy a simple wooden flower press from a craft shop or you can put the flowers between sheets of newspaper or blotting paper weighted down under heavy books. Make sure that the flowers are laid out absolutely flat in one single layer. Leave in a dry room with a minimum temperature of 10°C (50°F) for 3-4 weeks.

Cowslips (below) are a favourite country plant which used to grow wild in huge numbers. Now they are much less common. Like so many wild flowers, the cowslip is a medicinal plant.

spread around. If your aim is to create a cottage garden, this is less important, as a few flowers which have seeded themselves in unexpected places add to the natural, informal effect.

Whatever you do, do not dig up plants you see in hedgerows or in wild places. Apart from the fact that many of the plants are protected by law, they need all the help they can get to survive. Buy your wild flowers as seeds, bulbs or plants from a reputable nursery, then you can be sure you are helping to increase the species. If you are impatient to see the finished result, the quickest way is to buy small, partly-grown plantlets in spring or summer, which can be planted in a pot or straight into the garden when you get them home. Buy bulbs in the autumn and plant in exactly the same way as daffodils or crocus bulbs.

Garden Lighting

If you think your day in the garden ends when dusk falls, let us throw a little light on the delights of the evening garden.

Garden lights can transform your garden at the flick of a switch. You will see it in a new light, view your plants in a fresh way, and discover a quietly different garden after dark.

Garden lighting does not have to be restricted to unimaginative floodlights. Instead you can explore the possibilities of illuminated intimate corners to sit on a warm summer's evening, enjoying the company of friends and making the most of those plants whose heady fragrances often seem so much more powerful after dark, like honeysuckle, night-scented stocks and night-scented tobacco plants (so much more intoxicating than the varieties bred for daytime enjoyment). Use your imagination to pick out interesting features, create pools of light and darkness, and cast dramatic shadows.

Time to enjoy

Garden lighting is just as effective whether you like throwing parties or simply enjoying the quiet companionship of friends in pleasant surroundings. During the day you are likely to be tempted to work and improve the garden, but the evening gives you the opportunity to sit back, relax and enjoy the fruits of your patient labours.

Lighting effects are not just confined to the summer months. For instance, a spotlight on a striking plant in winter, perhaps the pale ghost-like bark of a silver birch or the spiky purple leaves of a coloured New Zealand flax (*Phormium spp.*) rising from a layer of pure white snow, will create an arresting view from the warmth of the house no matter how uninviting the weather.

Easy for anyone

Safety is, of course, a major consideration when using electricity out of doors. In fact, many systems operate on a low voltage from a transformer in the home, so the outdoor cables are perfectly safe. If you live in a very sunny area, you can buy solar-powered garden lights that are completely independent of your mains supply. Even some of the mains lights, which are generally the most powerful and useful, are relatively easy to instal and safe to use as long as you take a few sensible precautions.

If you want lights in permanent positions, such as decorative lanterns by the drive, or porch lights, you will need a qualified electrician to instal them. It is worth having some outside sockets put in at the same time so that you can use them for power tools such as the mower.

Good garden lamps, even when clearly in view, highlight plants and other notable garden features such as the raised circular patio and the impressive stone blocks embedded with plants (right).

The feathery fronds of fennel (below) are lit up by a single, dedicated lamp, showing how imagination, and a willingness to experiment, can show you aspects of your garden which may previously have been hidden from view.

DON'T FORGET!

THINK OF THE NEIGHBOURS

Keep on good terms with your neighbours. Make sure lights point downwards rather than upwards or over the fence and through their windows.

SECURITY LIGHTING

Lighting can make the garden safer. A floodlight over the patio can help prevent accidents. A small light set into the wall by a flight of steps will make it less hazardous after dark, and a good light without too many shadows by the barbecue can make burns and other accidents less likely.

As a burglar deterrent, if you are having an electrician install an outdoor lighting circuit, you could even consider having lights around the house that switch on automatically when they are approached, or that can be set to turn on and off on a time switch if you are out of the house.

If you have a number of power points in various parts of the garden you will be able to move your lights around with ease, always being sure to use the special waterproof sockets. Run the cable in a conduit buried at least 45cm/ 18in below the ground and cover it with protective tiles. This reduces the risk of tripping over trailing wires as well as the risk of electrocution.

Safety first

Waterproof connectors must *always* be used outdoors and are readily available from water garden suppliers, garden centres and electrical shops. With any kind of mains outdoor light, always use a circuit-breaker, which will protect you if the wires are accidentally cut.

Low-voltage lights can be used with complete confidence and installed without the help of a qualified electrician, which makes them a much cheaper option. The small transformer that comes with them is simply plugged into a mains socket indoors or in a garage, and only the low-voltage cable is taken outdoors. The instructions will be simple to follow and the lights can usually be installed in less than an hour.

Remember, though, that trailing cables in the garden can still be a hazard. Make sure they are tucked out of harm's way.

If you simply want a carnival or party atmosphere for a special occasion, electric lights can be dispensed with. Candles, lamps and flares create all the atmosphere and mood you need. As these are purely temporary, they lack many of the advantages of a

A lantern can be useful to illuminate dark areas of the garden, even in daylight. This lantern (above) gives a warmth and security to its surrounding foliage. It is important to choose a colour of glass to suit your own needs. Some gardens benefit from stronger orange glows, some from whiter tones.

An array of 'novelty' lamps, such as these fanciful toadstools (right), are now available. Chosen wisely, they can add interest to your garden. But plan your lighting with care before you invest and be sure you have space to lay the wires without disturbing your plants.

permanent lighting system but you can have the best of both worlds by installing electric garden lighting for its year-round appeal, and supplementing it with flares and candles to create the right mood for a summer barbecue.

Lighting your garden does not necessarily have to be prohibitively expensive. One or two well chosen lights can be just as effective as dozens dotted around the garden, which will probably create a distracting collection of highlights.

Using light creatively

To make the most of creative garden lighting, you need to choose the right kind of light for the right position. For a festive theme, strings of coloured lights, cascading in loops from a trellis or wall, or threading their way through the branches of a tree, may be all that is required, especially if supplemented with candles and flares.

Many low-voltage systems are intended to cast a beam of light over a limited area: 'mushroom' types on thin stalks are intended to cast a beam of light down on to low bedding or perhaps carpeting ground cover plants like heathers, while pencil-shaped ones are for illuminating the way, perhaps at the edge of a path, and casting a little general light on to the surrounding flowers. These are practi-cal and pretty, but in some gardens they may look too conspicuous during the day.

The most effective lights of all are spotlights that can be hidden behind shrubs or bushy plants. You do not see them during the day, and after dark they cast their beams to create startlingly beautiful effects. Most widely available garden spotlights have a spike that can be driven into the ground. Usually, they have swivel heads that can be repositioned to accommodate growing plants or cope with the changing seasons.

Choosing the angle

By turning the beam around, or altering its angle, you can highlight different plants as they come into flower, or pick out different 'architectural' shapes (like a contorted willow or a shapely *Fatsia japonica*) in the winter garden.

Another vital consideration is your choice of plants to highlight. Surprisingly, plants that may look terrific during the day can be disappointing in artificial light. A white flower will often stand out, though reds and blues can look muted and disappointing. Summer bedding is not always so striking by night either, so you need to experiment until you find groupings of plants that really do work when lit up.

Taking shape

Foliage plants, including those with variegated leaves, can be disappointing, but gold foliage or gold variegation can be striking. *Shape* is more important than colour after dark. A plain green hosta with big bold leaves like *H. sieboldiana* 'Elegans' can be more imposing than a prettily variegated one which you may prefer by day. Other border plants worth turning the spotlight on include bear's breeches (*Acanthus spinosus*), *Crambe cordifolia* with its massive sprays of gypsophila-like white flowers on stems 1.8m/6ft or more

A garden light can fit snugly among border plants and foliage (above). The elegant statue lamp (right) is intended to be part of the garden sculpture, adding to its effect.

Patio lights are essential for outdoor dining (below) or simply reclining on a summer evening on the patio. They are available in a wide range of types and styles.

high, and red hot pokers (kniphofias). Some of the big grasses such as pampas grass look good in autumn.

If you have a herb garden, angelica and fennel are ideal subjects, and both of these can be grown in borders and in gravel too.

Bold shrubs or those with a strong outline like the false castor oil plant *(Fatsia japonica),* phormiums, with their big sword-like leaves, hardy yuccas and the palm-like *Cordyline australis,* in areas where it is hardy, all look good bathed in light and also cast interesting shadows.

Lighting trees

Trees are often too large to illuminate effectively in a small garden, especially where stray light may annoy neighbours, but a small specimen tree like a corkscrew hazel or contorted willow will make a fine feature in winter.

Evergreen plants like the Australian gums (eucalyptus) show up well at any time of the year. It is not always necessary to illuminate the whole tree – the silvery-white trunk of a birch, perhaps set against a dark hedge, can create a splendidly dramatic effect.

Spotlights can be especially effective picking out an ornament or statue. A simple bust on a plinth, perhaps set in an alcove or backed by a brick wall, will look wonderful framed by plants like ivy and picked out in a spotlight.

Try moving a light around before you fix it, shining it from low and high angles, from first one side and then the other – all will affect the amount of detail revealed, and the effect of the moving shadows is a marvellous lesson in the use of lights.

A solar-powered unit (left) uses state-of-the-art equipment. Another boon is that it is entirely free of the mains system, which gives added flexibility and saves time in the installation. But take good advice from a reliable dealer or experienced friends to ensure that you have the right amount of sunlight needed to operate this equipment. Some gardens may receive enough natural light for only a few weeks every year. Many people do find solar units a very shrewd investment.

BRIGHT IDEAS

107

Climbers and Creepers

A climbing plant can do far more than just scale a wall. It is equally at home trailing from a tub, cascading over a bank or softening the outline of a garden ornament or statue.

Climbers are most commonly used to festoon trellises and pergolas with glorious summer flowers, or to embroider walls with leaves that develop rich autumn tints. Yet they can also play other exciting roles in a garden, if you don't think of them simply as 'climbers'.

In the wild, these plants sprawl and scale their way through life, greedily taking advantage of whatever support is available. In the gar-

den, however, climbers are usually provided with a support that both enables them to climb and contains their desire to wander further.

Spreading creepers

When a garden climber is not given support, it will either creep in search of something to climb up or will develop a sprawling and bushy nature. Some climbers, especially ivies, are quite happy to creep along the ground while those

with a woody nature usually spread outwards.

Climbers without supports have an unruly nature but they can be trained and used in many different ways, including carpeting an area under a tree, brightening a steep bank or clothing an unsightly tree stump.

Tubs and troughs

When grown in large tubs, climbers are free to trail and cascade, but not to spread or

Cloak a bank in a dense blanket of Persian ivy (above), which will spread on the ground to create a carpet of variegated colour. This Hedera colchica 'Dentata Variegata' has glossy green leaves with golden tinged edges.

Common ivy has been used to frame this statue (above right). Naturally it will creep horizontally and when something crosses its path, it will climb.

talis) at the tub's base, so that the blue or violet-blue flowers of the clematis grow down through the small, green leaves of the cotoneaster.

The orange-peel clematis (*C. orientalis*) should be planted in a large tub and the stems should be allowed to sprawl and cascade into nearby plants. It creates a spectacle of yellow, scented, bell-shaped flowers during late summer and early autumn. *Clematis tangutica* is similar, and also at its best when spreading into other plants.

Japanese honeysuckle

Japanese honeysuckle, *Lonicera japonica* 'Aureoreticulata', is eye-catching in any container, with its variegated green leaves with bright yellow veins and fragrant pale yellow flowers. Unfortunately, this evergreen plant is not suitable for extremely cold gardens.

On a smaller scale, trailing and sprawling annuals are superb for softening the silhouettes of troughs and window boxes. There are many trailing forms of climbing and upright annuals, including nasturtiums, lobelias, and begonias. These can be raised

Honeysuckle may seem an unusual choice for ground cover but it creeps along horizontally just as well as it climbs. Lonicera japonica 'Aureoreticulata' (above) is an evergreen variety.

If you plant a small growing clematis such as macropetala 'Maidwell Hall' (left) in a big stone jar and give it no support it will soon cascade over the side.

wander unduly.

Few climbers are more suited to this than Chinese clematis, *C. macropetala,* which normally grows to 3m/10ft when climbing up a trellis. In a tub, where its height is restricted to about 1.2m/4ft, its trailing stems will spread around the base of the container, softening the outline. The nodding, violet-blue, early summer flowers are followed by fluffy seed heads. The variety 'Markham's Pink' (also known as 'Markhamii') is less vigorous and ideal both in smaller tubs and for trailing over low walls.

Terracotta jars

Tall terracotta 'olive' jars are particularly suitable for growing clematis, enabling the plant's stems to trail freely and producing a very attractive display. Because clematis generally likes to have cool roots, position your container with an easterly or westerly aspect rather than one facing directly south.

The types of clematis best suited for containers are those with a cascading nature and a mass of stems. *Clematis alpina* is suitable but can look sparse unless grown with another plant. Try growing fish bone cotoneaster (*C. horizon-*

With its attractive herringbone shape and year-round display of colour, Cotoneaster horizontalis (left) provides a particularly effective covering for bare walls or banks. In early summer small pink flowers appear, followed by the characteristic rich profusion of bright scarlet berries. In late autumn the glossy dark green leaves turn a warm and glowing red. If you site this climber against a shady, sheltered wall, it can grow up to 2.5m/8ft high.

each year from seeds. If you have troughs on high walls or along the tops of flat-roofed garages or porches, these plants are a must. They will unify your display and hide the containers.

Cloaking walls

Low walls around front gardens can be stark and featureless unless partly covered with a few plants. Flowering shrubs that can be pruned to shape, such as forsythia and bridal wreath (*Spiraea × arguta*), are ideal for softening the outlines of garden gates, but low walls benefit most from cascading and trailing plants. The variegated greater periwinkle, *Vinca major* 'Variegata' (sometimes sold as 'Elegantissima'), has a vigorous sprawling and trailing habit that enables it to clamber over low walls, but for a more dominant yet still cascading nature the deciduous fishbone cotoneaster, *C. horizontalis*, is better. Although not classified as a climber it has a cloaking nature, spreading horizontally or vertically.

Garden steps can be improved in appearance by planting sprawling climbers at their sides. Common ivy (*Hedera helix*) is the easiest form to grow and forms a dense carpet of evergreen leaves and is suitable even if the area is heavily shaded. If your steps are in a sunny spot, however, you have far wider more colourful choices.

Variegated ivies are bright and include the Persian ivy (*Hedera colchica* 'Dentata Variegata'). If you have steps which pass through an arch as they connect two levels of the garden, this ivy will soon clothe the entire feature with green leaves edged creamy-yellow and with white overtones. The Canary island ivy (*Hedera canariensis* 'Gloire de Marengo') is also very attractive, with leaves variegated silvery-grey, creamy-white and green.

Ground cover clematis

Several clematis varieties are ideal for cloaking the ground, especially *Clematis × jouiniana* 'Cote d'Azur', a shrubby

Common ivy, Hedera helix (right), is one of the most useful climbing plants and can easily be grown as either a creeper or a bush. The young runners have aerial roots along the stem and will attach themselves to any surface you give them. When the runner reaches the top and cannot grow upwards any further, it will begin to form a bush with yellow-green flowers and black berries.

Ivies make wonderful ground cover and do an excellent job of filling in gaps and softening the appearance of straight edges. A sunny flower bed with plenty of light provides the perfect spot for the variegated 'Goldheart' (below), one of the many varieties of Hedera helix. Dark green ivies, on the other hand, will grow quite happily in dark areas of the garden.

climber with azure-blue flowers in late summer. Others include *C. tangutica*, one of the prettiest of the yellow-flowered clematis, which has brightly-coloured, lantern-like flowers from midsummer to early autumn, followed by fluffy silver heads, and *C. flammula* which bears white, fragrant flowers from late summer to autumn.

Highlighting statues

Positioning statues and ornaments in a garden is an art and one that should not be rushed. Large ornaments need to be seen from a distance, whereas small and delicate ones can create a surprise in a small garden, perhaps becoming apparent only after turning a corner.

Small statues can be enhanced by creating sympathetically coloured backgrounds.

Hedera helix 'Buttercup' (above) has light green leaves which turn a beautiful rich yellow in full sunlight. It is resistant to frost and makes an eyecatching splash of colour against a plain wall or among other evergreens.

The Japanese crimson glory vine, Vitis coignetiae (below), is a magnificent ornamental creeper. In the autumn its large green leaves turn all colours from yellow through orange and red to purple and crimson.

1-4ft high, then plant a climber to cloak it and turn it into a pretty feature.

Do not plant the climber too close to the stump, as the soil around the trunk will be impoverished and dry. A planting distance of 45-60cm/1½-2ft is about right.

As well as climbers, many roses are superb for smothering tree stumps with summer flowers. 'Aloha', for example, is a modern shrub rose with fragrant, double, rose-pink flowers. It will grow to a maximum height of 1.5-2.1m/5-7ft. 'Juno' is a centifolia type bearing large, blush-pink fragrant flowers, while 'La Ville de Bruxelles' is a damask rose with large, rich pink and very fragrant flowers. Both of these varieties grow to a maximum height of 1.5-1.8m/5-6ft.

Bank and walls

If your garden has a steep bank, you may find it difficult to cultivate. The soil is probably prone to being washed away by summer storms and, even if grassed over, you may find it awkward to mow. A

For instance, bright white statues can be too dominant amidst green plants, but when cloistered with a light-coloured background, and a white-flowered climber tumbling from a wall, they can create an aura of peace and tranquility.

Weathered statues are ideal when positioned against dark green plants such as yew. Alternatively, position them to be highlighted by the sky, with trailing plants around the base to soften the edges and to unify it with the surroundings. Do not use bright, variegated plants, as these detract attention from the statue.

Clothing tree stumps

Digging up an old tree stump is laborious. It is a task, however, that can be avoided. Leave the stump where it is, cutting it down to 30cm-1.2m/

ROSES TO SMOTHER THE GROUND

Many roses are superb as ground-cover, but do not grow them beneath densely-leaved trees or evergreens.
- 'Max Graf' has a spreading and low-growing nature. It rarely grows taller than 30cm/1ft. It has pink apple-scented flowers.
- 'Nozomi' grows to 30cm/1ft high and has a 1.5/5ft spread. It bears small, pink and white flowers.
- 'Snow Carpet' grows about 30cm/1ft high and has a 90cm/3ft spread. It has double, snow-white flowers.

If you're looking for ground cover but perfer the idea of fresh summer blooms to an ivy or vine, then a ground-sprawling rose could fit the bill. The delicate blush-pink flowers of 'Scintillation' (above) bring a fairytale feel to the garden while at the same time solving the problem of that awkward-to-mow area. Rambling and climber roses are not difficult to grow. Several species are so vigorous and thickly-flowering you can use them together with ivy or a vine to grow up the walls of your house.

sprawling or creeping climber could be the answer to your problem. A ground-sprawling rose, for example, will create a breathtaking feature which is also labour saving.

Roses that happily sprawl over banks and walls include 'Félicité et Perpetué' (creamy flowers with a primrose fragrance), *Rosa paulii rosea* (pink with white centres) and 'Scintillation' (blush-pink).

Old, weathered brick walls, perhaps already rich in shades of red and brown, can be further enriched by training a honeysuckle along the top so that the colourful clusters of summer flowers cascade at eye height. Plant the honeysuckle on the sunny side of the wall, preferably where the setting sun can light up the flowers during the evening. Fix supporting wires 10-15cm/4-6in from the top of the wall.

Rambling romance

If you have a rambling and informal garden, with perhaps an old brick shed or garage which has partly fallen down, do not write it off. It can probably be turned into a whimsical and unusual feature when draped with trailers and other plants. Paint the walls white and plant white climbers such as the densely-flowered and extremely vigorous mountain clematis (*C. montana*) to trail and cascade from the top. *Clematis armandii* 'Apple Blosssom' is also spectacular, less densely flowered but with the bonus of attractive leaves. If it is practical, plant your clematis on the opposite side of the wall, so that they appear to cascade over the top. Large areas of white wall tend to dominate the delicately-shaped, blue or violet-blue flowers of *Clematis alpina* 'Frances Rivis', so it is best to plant this variety against a grey background.

Long stretches of wooden fencing, especially when ageing, can be dull and uninteresting. Grow the vigorous climber 'mile-a-minute' vine (*Polygonum baldschuanicum*) to create a cascade of frothy, white flowers from the top of the fence from mid summer to

PERFECT PARTNERS

A swathe of clematis falling over a stone wall provides bright summer colour, set off by the Cornus alba 'Spaethii', commonly known as dogwood, planted in the bed at the foot. This attractive shrub with its golden variegated leaves gives support to the clematis in summer. In winter, its brilliant red bark stands out against the grey stone.

autumn. It is so vigorous – up to 3.6m/12ft of growth each year – that it can be planted at one end and allowed to scramble right along the length of the wooden fence.

Brightening hedges

Hedges that have become old and perhaps unsightly can be brightened by allowing the mountain clematis (*C. montana*) to sprawl over it. The white flowers, about 5cm/2in across, appear during spring.

Vigorous climbers can also look spectacular when clambering up the trunk and through the branches of a deciduous tree. Choose a climbing rose such as 'Cécil Brunner' with its thimble-sized, shell pink, slightly scented blooms, or 'François Juranville', whose glowing pink flowers are tinted with gold and are gloriously apple-scented. The Japanese glory vine (*Vitis coignetiae*) has large leaves that turn rich shades of orange, red, yellow and purple in autumn.

Honeysuckle (above), or woodbine as it is sometimes known, is one of our best-loved wild plants. In summer it bears pale yellow flowers tinged with purple-red, followed by bright red berries.

Rambling and climbing roses come in all shades and, trained over a pergola or tree (above right), will smother the bare wood in a frothy cascade of sweet-scented flowers to give your garden a delightful touch of old-world charm.

Quick-growing and easy to cultivate, clematis is one of the most popular climbers. A luxuriant fall of the spring-flowering Clematis montana 'Rubens' (right), transforms a featureless strip of plain board fencing into a mass of pale pink stars.

Brilliant Blooms

Fill every spare inch of your garden with summer bedding plants and their vibrant colours will provide a glorious display for months.

Most of us have a limited amount of time to spend in the garden, and this is where summer bedding plants can be such a boon to today's busy gardener. To make the most of them, plant them together in generous clusters to create a bold splash of colour rather than space them out along a border where the eye-catching effect of their colour will be lost. The hard work has already been done by somebody else so these half-hardy annuals, raised from seed in their containers, save you all the bother of providing heat and light, and of pricking-out and hardening-off. All you have to do is go to your nearest garden centre or market – or even a large supermarket – in early summer when sudden frosts are less likely, choose what you like, and plant it immediately. The result should be a display of massed brilliance which will last until the very end of the summer.

No trouble

If your garden is still at the early planning stage, you should leave half-circles, at least 45cm/18in deep, between other plants. Of course, the width very much depends on the size of your garden: if you have a very small garden, you will not want large areas left bare until the summer.

One solution for the spring and autumn months would be to grow small bulbs in these spaces. Use a trowel rather than a fork when planting out your bedding plants to avoid accidentally damaging the bulbs below the soil.

If you already have shrubs which are planted close together, with little room for anything else in between, you may need to move them. The best time to do this is in the autumn when they are dormant. If you want 'pockets' of flowers among your shrubs immediately cut shrubs back slightly. Few resent a little gentle pruning at the wrong time. Do remember, though, that their already established roots will take up any food you provide so water and feed the new arrivals very carefully.

Cheap and cheerful

The cheapest and most efficient way to buy bedding plants is in 'snap-off' strips of plastic or polystyrene. Each full set should contain around 10 annuals such as petunia, and the roots suffer less than they do in trays packed with around 40 plants where you have to prise more roots apart before you can safely plant them.

Never buy plants which are in full flower, and avoid lanky stems, discoloured leaves or any plants that have been reduced in price – these will not produce the best results. You should also avoid anything that has simply been lifted directly out of the ground and wrapped in newspaper.

Bright and bushy

Turn containers upside-down to make sure the roots are not growing through the bottom. Pick out plants that have good, strong stems with leaves near the base. Make sure they are bushy and are not packed closely, that they are all about the same size, and that the compost is moist.

A final word of warning about buying: quite a few growers, anxious to attract those who want something different, have bred spots and stripes into what were once self-coloured plants. These can look dramatic in a bed of their own in a large garden or in containers, but can be overpowering when grown in a small space with other plants,

Bedding plants can transform even the smallest garden (above). The pretty dazzling white fence contrasts brightly with the reds, yellows, greens and pinks of the flowers. Begonias, fuchsias and salvias offer interesting contrasts in shape and texture as well as colour.

A garden bursting at the seams with bright summer bedding can look absolutely spectacular. In this garden (left) bedding plants in pinks and white have been massed together to produce an explosion of colour.

Bedding plants in a wide range of colours contrast happily in this border (right). Buy them by the trayful as small plants and plant them where you want them to grow. Plant in groups rather than singly. The display will be blooming in no time and the beauty of it is that all the hard work has been done for you – no need to fuss over pricking out seedlings and hardening off.

so bear this in mind when choosing what to buy.

When you get your new purchases home, plant them immediately without worrying about your soil type as bedding plants are not fussy about where they live though many of them do well only in full sun. Now all you have to do is water them in and feed them – and sit back to await exclamations of amazement from friends and family who visit your garden.

Pretty popular

The following are the easiest and most popular half-hardies. Approximate heights are given to help the beginner plan the bed, but do not worry about spacing between them just mass the plants together.

African marigolds grow up to 3ft, though there are also dwarf varieties available.

If you stick to one colour the effect can be very pretty but you can stick to one family and still achieve a varied display. All the yellow plants (left) are tagetes (marigolds). The tallest are 'Lemon Gem', the middle are 'Inca' and the small blooms are 'Primrose Lady'.

A display of mixed petunias in purple, cerise and white (above) can create a delightfully simple effect. They are also good for containers.

be staked. The best type for general use are 'short' antirrhinums, which reach a height of about 22cm/9in. Mixed antirrhinums can be an astonishing sight, requiring little else for summer brilliance in small gardens – but the whole display can be ruined by an outbreak of rust disease. To avoid a season of disappointment, it is best to buy your plants from a reliable garden centre, and ask for rust-resistant varieties. Sometimes the plants last through

They have attractive, scented leaves in a range from pale yellow to deep orange.

Ageratum is also known as floss flower, and 'Blue Mink' is probably the most popular variety. Reaching a height of 20-25cm/8-10in, it produces fluffy blue flowers throughout

the summer and into early autumn. It also looks good when grown in containers with pretty white petunias.

Alyssum is a popular edging plant. The white varieties are best for this purpose because they provide a good contrast to a backdrop of taller, brilliantly coloured plants. Only 7-15cm/3-6in high, it tends to self-seed for the following year. You often see white alyssum combined with blue lobelia, in neat alternating clumps in a border. This can produce a rather regimented look, however, so avoid it if you want to create an effect of natural abundance.

Antirrhinum is commonly known as snapdragon. There are four sizes, ranging from 'dwarf', which are ideal for rockeries, to 'tall', that need to

PERFECT PARTNERS

GROWING TIPS

ALMOST INSTANT

Always keep a couple of packets of seeds – mixed cornflowers, pot marigolds (calendula) and mixed candytuft. Then, if anything fails, or if you find that you did not buy enough, you can still get almost instant colour. All you have to do is sow them thinly straight into the ground exactly as you want to see them grow. Cover them lightly and keep them moist.

the winter, but to avoid spreading any disease, it is best to remove them entirely after flowering.

Asters may have a short life, but the ones you can buy in early summer can do a lot to add a touch of colour to a drab corner. Available in attractive colours, these reach a height of 15cm/6in.

More favourites

Begonia semperflorens is a must in any bedding display. With red, pink or white flowers, often bronze-coloured foliage, and growing only about 17cm/7in tall, these well-tempered plants will brighten dull corners, tubs, window boxes and hanging baskets and do not even mind shade. It is best not to mix begonias with other brightly coloured half-hardies, as they will detract from each other. Use them in clumps in the border, as edging, or around miniature conifers in tubs.

Canterbury bell is a popular biennial which flowers for only three months and needs supporting. But, if you have room for it, by all means buy it

Bedding plants need not be planted in a mass. You can use them selectively just to pick out some features of your garden design. These dwarf busy Lizzies (right) are surrounding a pond, bringing life and colour to an otherwise dull stone edging. Although you may not normally match pink and red, with bedding plants anything goes!

LONGER LIFE

When frosts are forecast, do not desert your begonias or busy Lizzies because, with your help, they will continue to flower indoors all winter. Dig them up with a reasonable amount of soil attached and pot them up in soil-less compost in a pot just a little larger then the root ball. Snip out any withered, rotten, dead or diseased stems and trim the rest over lightly.

For a vivid contrast, fill a whole bed, or at least a large area, with a generous patch of shiny begonia semperflorens dotted with

iresine (left). Vivid purple heliotrope and silver-leaved senecio (above) are edged with a frame of geraniums.

for its attractive looks – perhaps in blue and white for a cottage garden look. It can grow to 90cm/3ft tall. Shorter varieties are available for rockeries, but these still need support.

Impatiens, or busy Lizzie, is the kind of good-natured, free-flowering plant that every busy gardener needs. Many people think of it only as a house plant, but gardeners have now seen its many advantages and are including it in the flower border. It will cheerfully go anywhere – under trees, in shady beds, in full sun – and will produce continual displays of brilliant colour. Its only disadvantage is that it needs a lot of watering. Busy Lizzie is available in many forms – plain, bi-colour, single, double, and even with variegated foliage. It reaches

about 15-23cm/6-9in tall, but has a drooping habit rather than remaining upright. One plastic 'strip' of perfectly plain plants is particularly useful for a tub on the patio, if your view from the sitting-room needs a bit of a lift in summer.

Lovely lobelia

Lobelia is probably most popular in its blue forms, and blue remains the favourite colour for edging flower beds or trailing from window boxes, hanging baskets or patio pots. Lobelia is a small plant, only growing to a height of 10cm/4in. If there is a bit of soil under the trailing varieties, you may find that they have seeded themselves and will flower again next year. They are especially useful for filling out hanging baskets, window boxes or containers, and can

look particularly lovely with just one other colour such as a pink ivy-leaved pelargonium (geranium).

Nemesia lasts for only a couple of months – much less than other annuals – but it would be a pity not to buy any because the mixed colours are so beautiful. The plants will tolerate light shade but, since they do not take kindly to a lot

of lime in the soil, you could use them with success on a patio in pots full of ericaceous compost. They grow about 25cm/10in tall, and should be cut back a little when the first flush of flowering is over.

Nicotiana (tobacco plant) smells marvellous on warm, romantic summer evenings. Some varieties close up during the day, but growers also pro-

Brilliant blooms transform a window box (above) and guarantee that the view from the window will be lovely. Lobelia, petunias and geraniums are used.

Take bedding plants to new heights with hanging baskets (below). Use geraniums, begonias and nasturtiums.

duce small varieties, with bright little faces, that remain open. These have no perfume, however, so are best avoided if you particularly want a touch of scent in your border. If you want that irresistible scent, then look for tall plants with white or pale green flowers; these produce rather straggly growth, though, so tuck them at the back of your bed.

Perfect pelargoniums

Pelargoniums, or geraniums, make excellent summer bedding and will overwinter indoors for next year. You can take cuttings from them very easily, too, and increase your stock further for a really colourful show. They grow to about 60cm/24in and come in white, pinks and reds, with many bi-coloured flowers and variegated or scented leaves.

Petunias are available in both striped and self-coloured forms. Stick to the latter if you mix them with other colourful bedders. They grow to about 20cm/8in and quite enjoy dry weather. The colours are wonderful, the flowers profuse, and the plants do not resent being gently chopped back if they become too straggly. They also propagate very easily.

There are, of course, other suitable bedding plants but these are the easiest to grow for 'instant brilliance'. With this 'shopping list' of best buys, you can add plenty of bright colours to your garden.

The Garden Path

Pretty and functional, paths that harmonize with the rest of the garden are a joy throughout the year. They are inexpensive and easy to create.

A path should harmonize with the part of the garden through which it passes, as well as complementing the style of the house. Plain concrete paths are ideal in vegetable gardens, where they have the functional role of enabling beds to be cultivated without the necessity of standing on the soil. In ornamental areas, though, you need to consider the path's appearance as well as its function.

Living in harmony

You also need to choose paths that harmonize with other features in your garden. Paths formed of pea-shingle, natural stone or slices of tree trunks are superb alongside rustic trellises, while paths constructed of regular-shaped paving are ideal with formal pergolas made of sawn and planed timber.

The design of a garden is often strongly influenced by the age and design of the house. Modern houses sit well with the angular outlines and bright surfaces of paving slabs, whereas those of the 1930s live happily alongside paths with softer outlines. Rustic cottages blend with paths formed of bricks, gravel and other 'natural' materials.

Fooling the eye

Some paths make the garden appear shorter or wider than it is. Paths made from materials that are 'natural' and harmonize with their surroundings tend to appear smaller, while those with sharp edges and regular sides, laid in straight lines, appear to cut through a

garden which makes them look large and dominant.

Natural materials

Paths formed from wood, pea-shingle, gravel, and natural paving create a restful feeling that unites the garden.

Make woodland and wild gardens easier to maintain, and add another visually exciting element, by placing slices of logs as stepping points through them. Keep plants away from the stepping stones by laying a rustic edging of 10-

A cleverly designed path can add interest to the small garden. This one (above) uses contrasting materials as well as varying widths. Curving the path behind a fence gives an illusion of depth to the garden.

15cm/4-6in wide logs. The area between the edging and the stepping logs can be filled in with complementary gravel. The edging logs enable flower beds to be raised slightly and the gravel provides a firm base for the logs.

Walking on water

Wooden bridges – or just stout planks – over shallow extensions of garden ponds or bog-gardens create attractive path-like features. Paths formed of natural stone, such as York paving, have an old and weathered appearance reminiscent of those sometimes found in cottage gardens but these tend to be very expensive. If you have inherited an old and overgrown garden and come across one of these paths, make a feature of it or lift and re-lay it in another place.

Grass can also be used to make a path and has the advantage of blending with all

plants. When you are laying a grass path, make it slightly wider than you think you will want it. Someone is bound to tread on the sides before the roots are established and by making it wider the edges can later be trimmed back.

Often, the edges of grass paths become worn and unsightly. If the path is straight, a row of square or rectangular paving stones can be set along the sides. If the path curves, an edging of crazy-paving is easier to instal, but the stones

An informal garden makes the perfect setting for a grass path (right). Let it flow in gentle curves with not a sharp angle in sight.

If your grass path gets a lot of wear, consider setting stepping stones down the middle (below left). Make sure the spacing is comfortable for all the family.

You can always mix and match the materials you choose for your path (below). Here a small patch of cobbles softens the formal effect of long lines of brick.

LAYING A BRICK PATH

If you choose brick for your path, avoid house bricks which freeze in winter and gradually break up. Frost-proof bricks look very similar but have a much harder surface. Tilt each brick slightly to provide a firmer foothold and angle them to let rainwater drain off the sides of the path. Laying the bricks 'frog down', with the flat face uppermost, uses fewer bricks than the more traditional 'on edge'.

Wood makes a very natural looking surface for a path (below), but it can become dangerously slippery in a damp area. Wood must always be set in a well-drained surface or it will soon rot.

will need to be cemented into position. Sometimes the paths become worn along their centres. They can be given an all-weather surface by setting paving slabs in them to act as stepping stones. These do not need cementing. Before setting the stones in their final position, space them out and ask members of the family to walk over them to ensure they are conveniently spaced for everyone.

Edging strips help to secure the sides. The crinkled-edged type looks best in an informal setting, while the straight edged ones are better in more formal gardens.

Man-made materials

For many generations house bricks have been used to create paths that exude weathered informality and old-world charm. However many house bricks are unsuitable for garden use and will quickly flake and splinter if exposed to wetting and freezing. Always make sure you buy special quality bricks, often referred to as engineering bricks.

If you want a brick path with mortar joints, you must use bricks, but if you prefer a brick effect with inconspicuous joints, use clay pavers. These look like bricks, but are thinner and are manufactured to a size that allows for bedding on a sand base without the need for mortar joints.

Both bricks and clay pavers can be bedded on sand alone, but you do need to use edging bricks or blocks mortared into position. Only bed a brick path on mortar over a bed of hardcore or concrete if it has to take a lot of heavy use.

Do not confuse clay pavers (which look like bricks) with concrete pavers (which are generally grey, reddish, or buff in colour). These are also bedded on sand, but they are thicker and provide a different kind of 'texture'.

Pre-cast concrete slabs are frequently used to create paths and these are available in a wide range of sizes and

Old quarry tiles set in a diamond pattern give this old concrete path a rustic look (left). The effect is further softened by the plants pushing up through cracks and tumbling over the sides.

Log slices make attractive stepping stone paths in wild or woodland areas (below). They must be allowed to dry out after cutting and then treated with a preservative as the end grain soaks up moisture from the ground very readily.

stepped on. Also, like pebbles, dirt collects around them and they need regular hosing.

Crazy-paving, formed from broken pieces of smooth-surfaced concrete slabs, is frequently used for paths. The paving itself has a formal nature, but used as crazy-paving it looks informal. Such paths, with the joints between each piece of paving at different angles, often appear shorter than they really are. They assume the contour of the ground and are more likely to become part of the landscape rather than ribbons on it.

geometric shapes (squares, rectangles, hexagonals, octagonals and circles). Surface textures range from smooth to rippled, and colours include grey, green, red, yellow and buff. They all have a formal nature and create paths with angular outlines and textures.

Paths formed of plain-surfaced materials with a normal concrete colour make superb walking surfaces and, as long as the area is not too large, they are fairly attractive. You can put pebbles between the slabs, or lay them in a sea of pea-shingle with concrete edging strips. Some people cement seashells between the slabs, but this is not always successful as shells are brittle and soon crack if

Hexagonal and octagonal paving slabs can be used to form unusual paths, their irregularly edged sides tending to give the impression of a shorter path, in contrast to straight-sided paths that are ideal for making short gardens appear longer.

Concrete pavers are roughly brick-sized but are usually shaped so that they interlock. They are laid on a bed of compacted sand which is also packed between the very narrow joints. They are resistant to damage from water and frost. There are several patterns in which they can be laid, some suited to paths while others are better for larger areas.

Running bond is simple to lay but because the pavers or bricks are normally laid across the path – rather than along it – a large amount of cutting is needed unless the particular blocks are available in half-sizes. Pavers laid across a path create a stronger surface than those laid along its length, especially at its edges. However, optically they have very different effects: a cross-pattern tends to make a path appear shorter, a lengthways bond makes it look longer.

Bring fragrance to your strolls by setting stepping stones into a camomile rather than a grass path (right). Every time your foot touches the leaves, it will bruise them and release a delicious scent. There's no need to tiptoe – camomile is tough enough to withstand a lot of wear and tear.

Small cobblestones can be very uncomfortable to walk on for any length of time unless they are set fairly deeply in mortar (below). These have all been angled to face in the same direction but variety has been introduced by laying a few rows at right angles at the turn and using smaller cobbles for the edges.

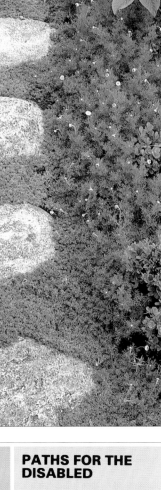

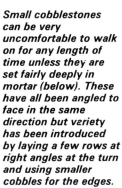

Parquet bond or basket-weave is easy to lay and the blocks do not need cutting if the width of the path is in multiples of the brick or paver size. Allow for joints in the case of bricks. Lay in squares formed of two blocks, side-by-side. The pattern produced by this bond is very attractive and does not confuse the eye into thinking the path is either too long or too short for the garden. These paths are however not always as strong as some other types.

Herringbone bond creates a strong, attractive surface with the bricks or pavers laid in staggered angled rows. This is not suitable for narrow paths, as a large amount of cutting is needed.

PATHS FOR THE DISABLED

Even-surfaced ramps beside steps are essential for easy wheelchair access. They should be wide enough for a wheelchair as well as someone walking alongside. The average width of a wheelchair is 50cm/20in so a path about 1.2m/4ft is needed. People who rely on walking sticks and crutches need regular and firm surfaces, while those with sight handicaps welcome a path where the surface texture changes at the edges to warn them when they are about to move off.

GARDEN NOTES

Trees for a Small Front Garden

Your front garden is the gateway to your home and a tree makes a deep-rooted first impression.
From flowering cherries to dwarf conifers, even if space is lacking there is a tree to grace your home. All it takes is a little careful planning.

Robinia makes an excellent standard, just right for a walled town house garden.

Magnolia is a hardy flowering tree. Its glorious blossom softens the lines of a modern house.

This Japanese maple is slow growing. Its outstanding autumn colour enlivens a plain lawn.

Think of your front garden as the first part of your home that friends will see; you will want it to look as smart and eye catching as possible and, ideally, it should require little maintenance.

A tree fits those priorities perfectly as it needs little upkeep yet gives a permanently changing focal point: perhaps clouds of blossom in spring, green foliage through the summer, possibly followed by fiery red leaves and bright berries in autumn and winter.

A bit of privacy

While the front garden itself provides privacy by spacing

Whatever the size of your garden, there should be a tree to suit. This pretty hybrid weeping Japanese cherry (Prunus 'Kiku Shidare Zakura') – above – grows to a maximum height of 6m/20ft.

Although slow growing, holly can be trained as shapely trees. Plant two for a touch of formal symmetry.

Here two easy-to-grow, hardy rowan trees reflect the balance of the house; red berries add bright spots of colour.

A crab apple echoes the country charm of a cottage with its pretty blossom followed by small fruits. Many grow no taller than 6m/20ft — perfect for a small garden.

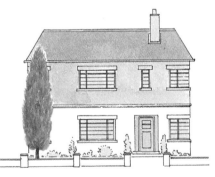

This tall conifer forms a narrow column which neatly complements the period features of the building. An evergreen, it will provide year-round interest outside a large house.

Japanese cherries are attractive ornamental trees which grow to a maximum height of 6m/20ft. Their dainty proportions are ideal in the front garden of a bungalow.

Many varieties of laburnum (right) are slow growing and reach a maximum height of 5.4m/18ft. The flowers are vibrant yellow and drape the branches in early summer. All parts of the tree are poisonous so be careful if you have small children.

THINK BEFORE PLANTING

DON'T FORGET!

● Trees are expensive to buy, so select wisely.
● Once established, a tree is difficult to move, so choose your site with care.
● *Always* check the maximum height and the spread.
● *Always* plant it far enough away from the house so that its roots will not undermine the foundations.
● *Never* plant a tree in frosty weather.

This weeping willow has become a problem because it has grown too large for the garden. Not only does the tree look out of place, it will also block the light to the house and may even damage the foundations. Too large a tree will also deprive other plants of food and water.

your house from the road, a tree can screen your garden from the outside world.

Before you rush off to the garden centre or nursery to choose your tree, however, do remember to check the eventual 'mature' size and shape of the young tree of your choice. The garden centre or nursery should advise you – and you can refer to the tree chart (over the page) which also includes helpful descriptions of flowers, foliage and berries.

Vital statistics

The size of your garden will determine the size of the tree you choose. A tree with a fast-growing spread could touch the house, overhang your neighbour's garden, or create too much shade, which will then prevent other plants from growing.

As well as above-ground growth, do not forget about activity underground. Poplars and willows in particular are the wrong choice for a small garden, as their roots will seek out any cracks and crevices in building foundations, in search of water. Instead of large and unsuitable trees like ash, beech, lime and oak, go for smaller evergreens such as junipers, attractive blossoming fruit trees or compact but impressive magnolias.

125

For new town houses with clean lines, Prunus 'Amanogawa' (left) fits the bill. Given fertile soil in a sunny position, it blossoms from March to May and looks outstanding in the smallest garden with its column-like growth. In contrast, 'Mount Fuji' (right) has spreading branches of snowy white fragrant flowers. A more traditional choice of cherry tree for an older house.

This compact, low-growing birch, Betula pendula 'Youngii' (below) has drooping branches that produce mustard-coloured catkins in spring. A deciduous tree, the leaves turn bright yellow in autumn.

TREE	VARIETY	HEIGHT
Acer (maple)	griseum	4.5m/15ft
Amelanchier (snowy mespilus, June berry)	lamarckii	3m/10ft
Cotoneaster	hybridus 'Pendulus'	2.4-3.6m/8-12ft
Juniperus (juniper)	chinensis	6m/20ft
Malus (crab apple)	floribunda	4.5m/15ft
Prunus (cherry)	'Amanogawa'	6-7.5m/20-25ft
Prunus	'Hally Jolivette'	4.5-6m/15-20ft
Pyrus (pear)	salicifolia 'Pendula'	2.4-3m/8-10ft
Robinia (false acacia)	pseudoacacia 'Frisia'	3-4.5m/10-15ft
Thuja	orientalis	4.5m/15ft

This crab apple bears fruits (left) which live up to its name – 'Golden Hornet' – and weigh down the branches in autumn. The cup-shaped flowers (below) blossom profusely in late spring.

A popular choice for year-round colour, Ilex aquifolium or common holly (bottom) bears bright red berries on glossy, spiked leaves. It reaches a height of about 6m/20ft.

SPREAD	FEATURES
2.4m/8ft	Deciduous. Beautiful bark and wonderful autumn foliage – red and scarlet.
3m/10ft	A bushy tree with white flowers and black berries.
2.4-3m/8-10ft	Red, yellow and orange leaves in autumn. Deciduous. Clusters of pinkish white flowers followed by red berries on weeping stems.
1.5m/5ft	Conifer. Range of foliage colours available, from yellow through bright green to blue-green or grey.
5.1m/17ft	Spreading; deciduous. Fragrant pink-white flowers and tiny green fruits that turn yellowy as they ripen.
1.8-2.4m/6-8ft	Tall and slim with masses of fragrant pink flowers and almost bronze coloured leaves.
4.5-6m/15-20ft	Small, graceful, willowy tree with semi-double white flowers.
1.8-2.4m/6-8ft	Weeping tree with cream flowers and small, silvery leaves.
2.4m/8ft	Feathery golden foliage keeps colour through summer. Deciduous.
3m/10ft	Evergreen domed tree. Mid-green foliage that turns bronze in winter. Other foliage colours available.

All in all, selecting the right type of tree for your front garden is very important – it also presents an exciting challenge.

Making a spectacle

For maximum visual impact in a small space, choose a tree that has several attractive features: pretty foliage is one consideration, but many species, such as acer, also have beautiful bark and bright autumn colour, others have blossom and fruit. Some trees have fragrant flowers or foliage, while evergreens give low maintenance, year-round interest.

A buyer's guide

Young trees can be bought in these three ways:

Bare-rooted specimens are grown in a nursery, dug up and transported without soil but with a damp material such as peat packed around the roots to prevent drying out. They must be planted during the winter months, while dormant. After buying the young trees, do not delay planting for more than a few days.

Root-balled trees are also nursery cultivated. The soil is left intact around the roots, which are then wrapped in sacking or polythene. After

CUTTING BACK

To reduce the size of an established tree, one of these methods can be used.

Coppicing: cutting a tree nearly to ground level, leaving a stump that produces vigorous, bushy growth. This method can be used for alder, ash, eucalyptus, lime, oak, poplar and sweet chestnut.

Pollarding: cutting a tree back to the main trunk. A pollarded tree is usually left at a height of 1.8m/6ft or more and pruned annually to keep it in shape and encourage healthy growth.

buying, keep the root ball moist and do not remove the wrapping until you are ready to plant. Plant the trees in the early months of autumn or in spring.

If you intend to plant your tree at any other time of year, buy a **container-grown** plant: one that has been raised from a seed, cutting or graft and potted on into the container in which it is sold.

Planting points

The larger the tree, the larger

PROJECT

PLANTING A TREE

Dig a hole larger than the root ball. Fill the bottom with 5-7cm/2-3in mixture of peat, soil and a handful of bone meal. Carefully remove the tree from its container, easing out any pot bound or very long roots and place it in the bottom of the hole, being careful not to break up the root ball. Place a stake into a hole alongside the root ball and hammer in securely. Fix tree to stake using tree ties, one near base of tree and one near the head. Fill the hole with more of the same planting mixture, firming in as you go. Water in very generously and apply mulch round base of tree. Keep a check on the firmness of the tree, particularly if there are strong winds.

Ivy, such as this Hedera helix 'Buttercup' (left) clothes a tree in a beautiful cascade of golden colour. The brightest of all the common ivies, be prepared to let it spread rapidly in its search for sun – the more sunlight the more buttery yellow its leaves become.

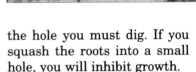
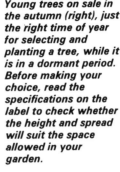

Young trees on sale in the autumn (right), just the right time of year for selecting and planting a tree, while it is in a dormant period. Before making your choice, read the specifications on the label to check whether the height and spread will suit the space allowed in your garden.

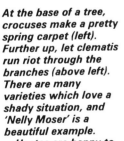

At the base of a tree, crocuses make a pretty spring carpet (left). Further up, let clematis run riot through the branches (above left). There are many varieties which love a shady situation, and 'Nelly Moser' is a beautiful example.

Hostas are happy to grow in the shade and make excellent perennial ground cover. The subtly variegated Hosta fortunei 'Aurea Marginata' (right) forms large leafy clumps.

the hole you must dig. If you squash the roots into a small hole, you will inhibit growth.

When planting a tree in a lawn, do not allow the grass to grow right up to the trunk. Allow 60cm/2ft around the base of the tree, keeping this clear of grass or other plants for the first two years, to allow the tree to establish itself.

Newly planted trees must be firmly staked for support. Put the stake in the ground close to the tree's roots *before* covering the roots with soil. Tie the tree loosely to the stake with a special stake tie. Check the tree regularly, especially in the event of strong winds, which may lift the roots.

Well-dressed trees

When buying an older house, you may be lucky enough to get a mature tree as well – but unlucky if it is too large, unattractive, dangerous or dead.

If you wish to keep the offending tree but would like to make it more of a feature, you could clothe it with a climber. Plant an ivy, clematis or rambling rose at the base of the tree and allow it to grow up and around the trunk and into the branches.

Pruning can improve the tree's shape and encourage fruiting and flowering.

129

A Low Maintenance Garden

If you are tired of spending more time working in your garden than you do relaxing in it, try replanning and replanting it on practical, labour-saving lines.

A low-maintenance garden can be just as attractive as one that takes hours of work every week – it is simply a question of how it is laid out, and the type of plants it contains. Invest a few hours in redesigning your patch, and a little labour to make the necessary changes, and you will have plenty of time to sit in a deckchair and enjoy the sight and sound of your neighbours toiling while you laze.

Trouble-free lawns

A lawn is usually the most labour-intensive part of the garden, demanding weekly mowing through the summer. It helps to reduce its size, especially by lifting odd bits and pieces, but do not be tempted to get rid of it altogether; a garden with nothing but hard surfaces can look rather bleak, especially in winter when the lawn provides the only large splash of green.

A lot of work can be saved by

Low-maintenance does not mean low interest. The combination of a lawn with conifers, shrubs and ground-cover plants (above) will provide year-round colour. Here the lawn, with its circular island bed, is the only feature that requires any regular attention.

One of the best ways to avoid work in the garden is to choose plants which perform year after year. The ground cover rose, 'Nozomi' (above) flowers in midsummer while the evergreen shrub Viburnum tinus (right) blooms in winter. Day lilies (Hemerocallis spp.) lend exotic flower shapes and a wide palette of colours to a border. The pink H. 'Cherry Cheeks' (below) is typical.

BRIGHT IDEAS

ROSE CARPETS

Ground cover roses are ideal in a low-maintenance garden, offering pretty flowers over a long period as well as suppressing weeds.

'Max Graf' has pink flowers in June-July, while the pearly pink blooms of 'Nozomi' appear in midsummer. The blood red flowers of 'Fiona' appear repeatedly.

Varieties in the 'Game bird' group are specially bred for ground cover. 'Grouse' and 'Pheasant' are pink, and 'Patridge' is white. All three are repeat flowering.

choose a rotary mower rather than a cylinder model. This will cope with grass up to a foot high without flattening it. Set the blades high and collect the cuttings in the box or by raking. They can be used as a weed-suppressing mulch on the nearest flower bed.

As a general rule, do not cut the grass too short – this only makes more work, as a scalping encourages faster growth. Leave it about 2.5cm/1in long.

Tackle the time-consuming chore of neatening the edges by eliminating them as much as possible. Remove any island beds, and have paving stones or paths running along the lawn edge wherever possible. Stop grass roots from creeping into the flower beds by digging the earth back, or by confining the lawn with corrugated plastic edging strip. An adjustable electric lawn edger is an excellent investment, useful for mowing difficult areas around trees and close to fences.

Finally, do not put fertilizer on your lawn – this makes it grow faster. Clover, daisies and other small plants can be left where they are. Get rid of large weeds like dandelions by rubbing their leaves with a touch weeder rather than by digging them out.

Hedges

Formal hedges needing close clipping, such as privet, can be hard work. If you already have

altering the shape of the lawn. An area with straight or gently curving edges is the easiest to mow; avoid making intricate, fussy shapes.

Make sure you have the right mower. For a small lawn, a lightweight electric mower should do the job in no more than about 20 minutes. Do not bother to use a grass box; unless the grass is very long the clippings will simply disappear into the ground and help to nourish the lawn.

If you cannot manage weekly mowing, make sure you

SHORT CUTS

WATER COVER

An informal pond is very low-maintenance. The larger the area it takes up the better, as the expanse of water needs no regular attention – all you do is sit and watch the fish. Site it well away from trees, to avoid a fallen-leaf chore in autumn, and put in plenty of floating pondweed (hornwort) to oxygenate the water and keep it clear and free of blanket weed.

131

one, reduce its height so there is less to be done, and invest in powerful electric hedge clippers, or spray on a growth inhibitor in late spring.

Avoid planting new hedges. Grow screens of evergreen shrubs instead, or plant a shaggy, informal hedge that is only pruned once a year. There are many suitable plants – *Viburnum tinus* gives you winter flowers if you prune in spring, and *Berberis thunbergii* 'Atropurpurea' has beautiful purple leaves that redden in autumn.

War on weeds

The constant battle against weeds is always a chore. Chemicals help to a certain extent, especially on paths and patios, where one application of a long-acting weedkiller in spring should keep them clear all year. For beds, however, a long-term, three-pronged campaign is needed.

Weed early in the year before the plants get a hold, let alone set seed. The old gardeners' saying, 'One year's seeding – seven years' weeding!' is, unfortunately, all too true.

Cover the ground with close planting so that weed seedlings get no light. Ideally, have no bare earth visible.

Mulch areas that need to be bare – around the base of rose bushes or young shrubs. Bark chippings are ideal, as they are dark brown and look very presentable, but you can also use grass cuttings, garden compost and rotted manure. Aim for a depth of about 5cm/2in to stop weed seeds germinating from below.

If things get away from you, at least cut or pull off the flower heads of weeds before they set seed, to reduce the future damage, or use a contact weedkiller. A flame gun is the weapon of last resort in such

Rose of Sharon (Hypericum calycinum, above) is a free-flowering evergreen perennial, often used for ground cover; its use here as a low hedge is exceptional. Hydrangeas are also reliable perennials. H. macrophylla 'Blue Wave' (below) produces its lace-cap blooms from mid to late summer.

Dark brown bark chippings make a harmoniously-coloured and effective weed-supressing mulch in borders (above).

The silver leaves of lamb's ears (Stachys lanata) are evergreen and look well with varieties of sedum (below) such as 'Autumn Joy' and low-growing 'Lidakense'.

situations. Avoid rotovators; they chop up the roots of pernicious plants like bindweed and every little bit grows.

Labour-saving plants

Trees and conifers are the most maintenance-free plants of all, as once established they need no attention whatsoever.

Flowering shrubs are also good, but choose carefully. Make sure they are hardy in your district, suitable for your soil if it is noticeably acid or alkaline, and do not require regular pruning. Allow them plenty of room to develop their full height and spread, or you will end up having to set aside time to prune them regularly to fit their space.

Displays of rare and exotic plants in garden centres can be tempting, but for low maintenance keep to tried and tested favourites like forsythia, kerria and ribes (flowering currant) for spring flowers, and lilac, philadelphus (mock orange), weigela, potentilla, deutzia and hydrangea for summer flowers. Members of the large cotoneaster genus are invaluable for evergreen leaves and bright berries.

Spring bulbs, once planted, need little work. Leave them in the ground after flowering; just remove the dead flowers, to stop seed from setting, and let the foliage wither.

Hardy perennials

A garden composed entirely of shrubs underplanted with bulbs is the most labour-saving of all, but most people like to have some hardy perennial flowering plants as well. Cut down the work here by avoiding tall ones, such as oriental poppies, achilleas and delphiniums, that need staking. Steer clear, too, of large-flowered dahlias or chrysanthemums, carnations and gladioli, all of which need plenty of attention and/or staking.

There is no shortage of medium-height, trouble-free perennials, but some of the best are bear's breeches (*Acanthus spinosus*), Japanese anemone (*Anemone × hybrida*), *Astilbe* hybrids, fleabane (*Erigeron*), hellebores, day lilies (*Hemerocallis* spp.), hostas, red hot pokērs (*Kniphofia* spp.), catmint (*Nepeta mussinii*), lungwort (*Pulmonaria* spp.), leopard's bane (*Doronicum* spp.) and ice plant (*Sedum spectabile*).

Evergreens

To avoid bare soil and a bleak winter outlook, always include some flowering evergreens in a herbaceous border. Hardy specimens include the shade-loving, pink or white London pride (*Saxifraga umbrosa*), the silver-leaved, magenta-flowered lamb's ears (*Stachys lanata*), blue or white bellflower (*Campanula persicifolia*) and the low-growing, snow-white perennial candytuft (*Iberis sempervirens*).

Annuals brings welcome col-

CONTAINER COLOUR

Growing plants in containers is not labour saving if you have to look after them as well as mowing, weeding and trimming the hedge. However, they have their place in the low-maintenance garden, providing spots of bright colour among the prevailing green. And what could be pleasanter 'work' on a warm summer evening than sploshing water around and doing the dead heading from the comfort of your deck chair on the patio?

GARDEN NOTES

PAVING PROBLEMS

Weeds growing between paving stones get a tenacious grip and are hard to get rid of. Eliminate them by one of two methods.

Spray with long-acting weedkiller in spring and leave bare.

Plant creeping, self-seeding plants in the cracks and remove weed seedlings until the plants you choose fill the spaces.

GARDEN NOTES

our to the summer garden, but bedding them out can be time-consuming. Plant hardy cottage garden favourites such as love-in-a-mist, pot marigold, candytuft, godetia, gypsophila, cornflower, clarkia, larkspur and nasturtium; all will seed themselves and reappear regularly each year with no futher effort on your part.

Summer watering

Watering can be tiresome – but only if you make it so. Unless the summer is exceptionally hot and dry, it is best not to water. It takes hours to soak the ground to any depth, and sprinkling the surface merely encourages shallow root growth, making plants more vulnerable to drying out if watering is not continued. Never water a lawn. Even if the grass turns brown in the heat, it will recover amazingly quickly.

The only things that must have water are plants in containers, which dry out quickly, seedlings, and new shrubs, roses or trees that have not yet put down deep roots. Large plants benefit greatly from a mulch to stop surface evaporation. When watering them, use the spout of the can, not a rose, and give each plant a good gallon of water.

Room for roses

Most roses are hardly trouble-free, requiring careful pruning and being martyrs to aphids,

black spot and other ills, but you can still incorporate some in a low-maintenance garden.

Mulch round the base of existing bushes to conserve water and smother weeds. Spray at the first sign of aphids, before they get out of hand, and either pick off and destroy leaves afflicted with black spot, or live with it. Prune lightly, just enough to keep the bush in shape – hard pruning is done to encourage large flowers.

If buying new roses, choose shrub roses rather than hybrid teas (large-flowered bush roses), floribundas (cluster-flowered bush roses), climbers or ramblers. They can be left unpruned, and some are more resistant to disease. Look for a modern shrub rose such as 'Ballerina', whose fragrant pink flowers appear all summer, or old favourites like 'Cecile Brunner', which bears tiny pink flowers of enormous charm. Another good one is the pink-flowered rugosa 'Frau Dagmar Hartopp', considered by many experts to be the ideal rose – disease free, repeat flowering, and strongly scented, with large red hips.

In a small town garden, an enormous amount of work can be avoided by laying pavers or stone paths as a base for flowering perennials rather than the more traditional grass (above).

Shrub roses are the best choice for low-maintenance gardens. They do not have the large, spectacular blooms of some hybrid teas or floribundas, but they require much less attention and the best of them, such as 'Cecile Brunner' (left) bear masses of delicately coloured and scented flowers.

Dry and Shady Corners

Nearly every garden has a dry and shady corner but it need not be a problem area. There are many plants that will grow well in such conditions.

In sunny, open situations most plants thrive and put on a colourful display. Somewhere in your garden, however, there is bound to be a dry, shady area, under a tree, perhaps, or hard by a north-facing wall, where stunning colour is difficult to achieve. There is no need to despair; many plants will thrive in dry shade and turn problem areas into attractive focal points.

Woodland carpet
A ground-hugging carpet of foliage transforms dry shade under trees into an attractive woodland setting. It also suppresses weeds, which seem to prosper in any conditions. Ivy, a true woodland sprite, comes into its own in dry shade.

Variegated ivies such as *Hedera helix* 'Goldchild' and 'Glacier' will make a dash for areas of dappled shade, while common ivy, with its glossy green leaves, provides romantic, old-fashioned cover. For a lighter green ground cover and curly leaves grow *H. helix* 'Manda's Crested'.

Periwinkles, with glossy, light green leaves and soft blue flowers, cover dry, shady ground very quickly. There are variegated forms of both *Vinca major* and *V. minor*, but like variegated ivy they can only tolerate light shade.

Shady perennials
Many perennial plants are at home in dry shade. In spring, epimediums provide dainty

Dry shady conditions suit plants which grow wild at the edges of woodland, such as foxgloves (above).

Ivies are lovers of woodland conditions, including dry shade, and will bring colour and texture to spots where few other things will grow. The leaves of Hedera helix 'Manda's Crested' (left) turn coppery as winter approaches.

Various forms of spurge (Euphorbia spp.) grow well under trees, whence their cup-shaped golden-yellow bracts glow enticingly during the spring (right).

RECOMMENDED VARIETIES

Ground cover
Hedera helix 'Goldchild' has golden variegation and 'Glacier' has creamy-white edged leaves. *Vinca minor* and *Vinca major* have attractive glossy green leaves and pretty blue flowers.

Perennials
Stinking hellebore (*Helleborus foetidus*) has dark, deeply divided evergreen leaves, and green, bell-shaped flowers with maroon rims in spring. Euphorbias offer good stem colour and masses of bright golden-greeny flower heads. *Geranium phaeum* and *Geranium macrorrhizum* have mounded foliage and purple to magenta flowers in summer. Lady's mantle (*Alchemilla mollis*) has furry leaves and yellow-green flowers. *Heuchera sanguinea* 'Bressingham Hybrids' have reddish pink flowers, and need dappled shade.

Shrubs
Spotted laurel (*Aucuba japonica*) has evergreen spotted golden leaves. Females bear red berries in autumn.

Climbers
Climbing hydrangea (*Hydrangea petiolaris*) is deciduous, but has good foliage and pretty flower panicles. Persian ivy (*Hedera colchica* 'Sulphur Heart') has large floppy leaves with good bright colouring. Winter-flowering jasmine (*Jasminium nudiflorum*) has fragrant yellow flowers in spring.

Ferns
Cretan brake (*Pteris cretica*) has yellow-green, deeply divided fronds and grows to 45cm/18in. It needs winter protection. Rusty back fern (*Ceterach officinarum*) has fronds with rounded lobes and is semi-evergreen. The scales on the lower surface of the fronds mature from silver to bronze. It grows to 15cm/6in and suits the front of a shady area.

Bulbs
English bluebell has nodding stems of tubular blue flowers in spring. Lily-of-the-valley (*Convallaria majalis*) has pretty and fragrant flower bells carried on arching stems in spring.

white or yellow flowers, carried above mounds of heart-shaped foliage. The spring leaves of some epimediums boast splendid bronze tones. Put these low-growing charmers at the front of a woodland planting under trees.

Stinking hellebore (*Helleborus foetidus*) enjoys a similar habitat. It carries its deeply divided dark green leaves all through the year, and in late winter to spring produces heads of small, bell-like, pale green flowers with a maroon rim. They grow to 45cm/18in, with a similar spread.

Wild wood flowers
Euphorbias are also useful under trees. Wood spurge (*Euphorbia amygdaloides*), in its form *rubra*, offers bright red stems, dark, evergreen foliage and the brightness of massed yellow-green flowerheads in spring. Plants grow to a height and spread of 30cm/1ft. Also suitable is *E. amygdaloides robbiae*, a shorter plant with looser flowerheads of light green bracts.

Foxgloves (*Digitalis* spp.) give a natural-looking woodland effect under trees. They self-seed abundantly, and carry colourful flowers on lofty, long-lasting spikes.

Various cranesbills (*Geranium* spp.) make good ground-covering growth and produce pastel-coloured flowers. *G. macrorrhizum* has light green foliage and magenta summer flowers. Mourning widow (*G. phaeum*) carries its dark purple summer flowers above a light green foliage.

Lady's mantle (*Alchemilla mollis*) provides soft, furry foliage mounds and dainty yellow flowers in summer, while equally delicate flowers, in shades of red and pink, are of-

UNDER EVERGREENS

In the shade of evergreen trees, ferns are a good choice. Oak fern (*Gymnocarpium dryopteris*) quickly covers the ground with its rosettes of tall, feathery fronds.

A prickly evergreen butcher's broom (*Ruscus aculeatus*) is another suitable candidate for this situation. It produces small white flowers followed by bright red berries and grows to about 45cm/18in.

GARDEN NOTES

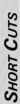

Good sources of floral colour in dry shady conditions include the magenta blooms of the delightfully dainty *Geranium* macrorrhizum *(above), here pictured with Solomon's seal (Polygonatum),* and the fresh greens of the stinking hellebore *(Helleborus foetidus, left).*

DRY START

Under deciduous trees, plant ground cover in autumn when the leaves have fallen. The ground cover plants will have a good start in relatively warm, moist soil with good light.

By the time the leaves are out again in spring the ground cover will be well established.

fered by heuchera (*Heuchera* 'Bressingham Hybrids'). Plant them at the outer edge of the tree canopy, as they are best in dappled or partial shade.

Shrubby shade-lovers

Various forms of spotted laurel (*Aucuba japonica*) provide glossy evergreen leaves in plain green or with golden variegations. If both male and female plants are planted, the females will bear bright red berries in autumn.

In the dry shade of walls or buildings, where indirect light is not restricted, variegated or

PLANTING UP A SHADY AREA

Use periwinkle and variegated ivy as the basic ground cover plants, with three or four plants for every square metre.

At random, in the middle of the planting area, set stinking hellebore, lady's mantle and mourning widow. Their foliage will rise above the ground cover and they will give a succession of flowers from early spring through to summer.

Towards the front, plant bulbs and lungwort (*Pulmonaria saccharata*) with its spotty evergreen leaves and pretty spring flowers. Combined, they provide early spring colour.

For autumn colour, plant white and pink flowered Japanese anemone (*Anemone japonica*). This tall-growing perennial carries its pastel flowers high on thin stems.

evergreen hollies make a bold splash of foliage colour.

On a shady wall or at the foot of a tall tree, plant the climbing hydrangea (*Hydrangea petiolaris*). Although it is deciduous, its spring and summer foliage and flowers make an attractive display.

Upwardly mobile

Ivies, too, can be used for upward cover in dry shade. For large, floppy, variegated leaves grow Persian ivy (*Hedera colchica* 'Sulphur Heart').

Winter-flowering jasmine (*Jasminum nudiflorum*) bears bright yellow flowers on leafless stems in the winter, and dark green leaves through the summer. It will need support.

Ferns

Many ferns will grow well in dry and shady situation, providing attractive shapes and delicate foliage.

Cretan brake (*Pteris cretica*), rusty-back fern (*Ceterach officinarum*) and fishtail fern

Despite the restricted choice of plants, simple planting schemes can still grace a dry and shady spot (above). Here, a bed of bluebells dominates the scene, with Solomon's seal providing height at the back; the latter's greenish-white flowers emerge just after the bluebells have passed their best.

The evergreen leaves produced by heucheras make good ground cover, but they are usually grown for their summer flowers. Those of H. 'Red Spangles' (left above) are particularly colourful.

Most ferns enjoy wet conditions, but some can cope with a drier site. Among the best are Pteris cretica 'Major' (left), with its pale green wavy fronds, and Ceterach officinarum, with leathery, dark green, lobed foliage (below).

GARDEN NOTES

FOOD AND DRINK

Before planting up the dry shady area prepare the ground so that the plants have the best start in life possible.

In autumn, dig the soil over and remove perennial weeds. Ground cover suppresses annual weeds but the perennial thugs need to be dug out.

Add bulky organic material to the soil and plant up the first layer of ground cover plants.

As you plant the areas up, water in well and mulch if possible. Keep plants well-watered during their first growing season, and in the case of shrubs, for the second growing season as well.

Once the plants are well-established, even though the conditions may not seem favourable, these specially chosen dry shade lovers will grow well.

BRIGHT IDEAS

ELEGANCE IN THE SHADE

Grow the elegant shrub *Garrya elliptica* with its glossy evergreen leaves and greyish-green, long tassel-like flowers. It provides subtle winter textures and combines well with the winter-flowering jasmine.

(*Cyrtomium falctatum*) offer interesting foliage in varying shades of green.

For a completely different effect, grow *Phyllitis scolopendrium* 'Crispum' with its upright, ribbon-like leaves. Common polypody (*Polypodium vulgare*) suits a shady area in a rock garden.

Bulbs

Many spring and autumn bulbs will provide generous displays that brighten up the dullest corners of the garden.

A traditional woodland favourite is the spring-flowering English bluebell. Its arching stems of soft blue, tubular flowers make a breath-taking display when massed in large clumps. Also useful is the shorter-growing Spanish bluebell or scilla.

Spring flowering lily-of-the-valley (*Convallaria majalis*) and Solomon's seal (*Polygonatum* spp.) will produce delicate flowers in poor conditions.

Hardy autumn and winter-flowering cyclamens do well in dry shade but need shelter from cold winds. Their marbled leaves will provide interest for much of the year.

Shady retreat

Include a seat of wood or iron so you can enjoy your shady glade as a quiet retreat from the brighter, more showy parts of the garden.

Planting up the shady area will be challenging, but the resulting combination of foliage colour and texture with subtle flowers will make a tranquil haven on hot days.

Architectural Plants

Grown for their bold shapes, architectural plants are often quite large, but just one or two can work wonders in the smallest garden.

Generally speaking, architectural plants are grown more for the striking beauty of their form than for colourful flowers. Many have stiff, upright leaves, suggesting a construction rather than a plant; others have leaves of large size or unusual shape.

Ideally, an architectural plant should also be evergreen, so that it is a permanent feature of the garden, not a seasonal event. The yucca is a classic example, with its tall sword-like leaves standing sentinel right through the year. Many architectural plants are tall, so that they stand out from the rest of the planting, but for the small garden there are plenty of more suitably sized but equally dramatic plants.

The average garden is designed on the general principles of the cottage garden, with borders packed as full of plants as possible. Usually, not much thought is given to their outline or leaf shape.

The result may be likened to an impressionist painting, full of drifts of colour but generally lacking in bold shapes, and often does not have much height to it. A garden designed on strictly architectural principles will contain far fewer plants, so that each one can be appreciated individually. It will be interesting all year round, but rather restrained – never a riot of colour.

Such plantings are generally most successful when carried out in small spaces that resemble outdoor rooms, furnished with paving, low walls, brick planters and tubs. They also have the virtue of being

labour saving, as the planting is confined to small, well-defined areas that are easy to look after.

For most gardeners, love of colour will prevent them from going all out for a truly architectural garden. However, there are two ways which architectural plants can be of great value in a more conventionally designed garden.

First, they can be used as accents – the horticultural equivalent of an exclamation mark – to give added interest to flower borders. Second, they can provide what our beloved roses, herbaceous perennials and gaily coloured annuals cannot – winter interest. Alternatively, you can grow

single architectural plants in handsome pots as a change from the usual annuals.

Familiar faces

Some of the best architectural plants are herbaceous perennials, once a familiar sight in gardens, that have been displaced by others with more showy flowers. Good examples are two prickly leaved plants, the globe thistle (*Echinops*) and sea holly (*Eryngium*).

Globe thistles are named for their perfectly ball-shaped flowerheads, in lovely shades of steel blue, standing singly on tall stems above a mass of large, deeply divided grey-green leaves. Sea holly has blue, teasel-like flowerheads,

Architectural plants are chosen for their dramatic outlines and sculptural shapes. This does not mean that they are all colourless. The flower heads of the long-stemmed kniphofia, for instance, are particularly warm and vibrant. This one (above) is K. rooperi.

The cardoon (Cynara cardunculus, right) is closely related to the artichoke. A native of the Mediterranean, where its leafstalks are eaten like celery, it needs protection from frosts, but given that produces handsome clumps of much-divided leaves with a grey-green flush (right) and large, thistle-like summer blooms.

All plants in the Cordyline *genus have good architectural qualities, but their use is restricted by a tendency to tenderness.* C. australis, *the New Zealand cabbage palm, is slow-growing, and makes a good container subject for a patio. All varieties produce a fountain of lance-shaped leaves; several, such as 'Torbay Red' (left) have unusual colours.*

surrounded by a big ruff of spiny grey bracts. Both are as tough as they look, and will survive in poor soil, frost and even a drought.

A relative of the globe thistle (they are both knapweeds), the globe artichoke (*Cynara scolymus*), although mainly grown to eat, also makes a striking border plant. It has large, much-divided, greyish-blue foliage, and thistle-like blue flowers above the handsome green bracts, which are the part normally eaten.

Another old favourite, grown for its stately, column-shaped heads of yellow-green, long-lasting bracts is spurge (*Euphorbia*). This is another good plant for poor soils. The tall ones are *E. characias* (often evergreen) and *E. c. wulfenii,* both reaching 1.2m/4ft.

Building with colour

Some popular herbaceous perennials, grown for their beautiful blossoms, also qualify as architectural or accent plants because they flower on tall, upright stems. The outstanding

*Globe thistles (*Echinops spp.*) are named for their ball-shaped flowerheads, carried on tall, slender stems.* E. ritro *(below) has, as an added attraction, deeply divided leaves that are noticeably downy on the underside.*

short-lived and need staking, but are well worth the effort.

Another tall and stately plant is the strange-looking red-hot poker (*Kniphofia*). The sturdy spikes of tubular flowers rising as high as 1.8m/6ft from grassy foliage, are usually yellow, with hot red or orange tips. But, if these do not appeal, they can also be obtained in cooler cream, yellow and greenish yellow.

Good for shady beds are monkshood (*Aconitum* spp.), with tall spikes of helmet-shaped flowers, commonly violet-blue, and robust glossy leaves, and the biennial foxglove (*Digitalis* spp.), with tall spikes of large tubular flowers in many colours, attractively spotted inside.

Tropical look

Some of the most striking architectural plants are ones with stiff, swordlike, spiny leaves which give them an exotic, tropical look. The yucca family includes some of the hardiest and handsomest.

There are numerous varieties, but all form a dense clump of bayonet-like, shiny green or variegated leaves

example must be garden or Russell lupins, with their showy spikes in white, yellow, orange, red-purple and blue, raised above large leaves evenly divided into fingers. They flower early, but are not long-lived, and prefer lime-free soil.

Equally popular is the delphinium family, traditionally grown for its magnificent rich

Lupins are another good way of adding summer colour to an architectural design. The 'Russell Hybrids' (above) are particularly suitable, throwing their multi-coloured racemes up to 1.5m/5ft above a border.

blue flower spikes, though these can also be pink, mauve, yellow, red or white, often with a contrasting dark eye known as a 'bee'. The most suitable as accent plants are varieties of *D. elatum*, which grow up to 2.4m/8ft. Delphiniums are

The sea hollies (Eryngium spp.) combine divided, well-coloured leaves with strong shapes and attractive, thistle-like flowers and bracts. E. giganteum (right), with its silver-grey stems, bluish flowers and shiny bracts, is a particularly fine example, but does not live as long as others in the genus, dying after flowering.

60cm-3m/2-10ft high, some razor sharp, others edged with curly white fibres. The spectacular spikes of large, creamy-white, bell-like flowers may take some time to appear, but should come annually thereafter if the plant is in full sun, not every seven years as sometimes alleged.

A similar, but slightly less hardy plant is New Zealand flax (*Phormium tenax*); protect it with mulch if it is left outdoors in winter. It may produce rusty red, tubular flowers, followed by curved, scimitar-like seed pods up to 10cm/4in long. The species has olive green leaves, and there are many variegated varieties, some in stunning solid shades of red and purple, others striped green and yellow.

Tall grass

Grass does not sound very architectural, but several tall, ornamental grasses make splendid architectural-style centrepieces for lawns or circular beds.

Perhaps the most popular is pampas grass (*Cortaderia selloana*). Its arching, grey-green, saw-toothed leaves grow up to 1.8m/6ft long, and are evergreen except in very cold districts. In late summer, the clump throws up huge

Pampas grass (Cortaderia selloana) has a delightful shape, with its clumps of arching leaves overtopped with a mass of billowy plumes. It makes a fine specimen plant year round, but is particularly valuable in the winter, when a dusting of frost or snow makes its flower heads even more imposing (above). Zebra grass (Miscanthus sinensis 'Zebrinus', right) is no less imposing, but, by contrast, is at its best in the summer, when its variegated leaves put on a spectacular show, and in autumn, when it produces flowers in the shape of loose panicles of white spikelets.

feathery plumes of creamy-white flowers on tall stout stalks, which sometimes last until the following spring.

Some of its varieties, such as 'Pumila', are smaller and more compact, better for a small garden. 'Rendatleri' has beautiful, purplish-silver plumes. Wear gloves when removing any dead leaves from the clump as they are razor-sharp.

Another tall, impressive-looking plant is silver grass (*Miscanthus* spp.). One of the most attractive species, zebra grass (*M. sinensis* 'Zebrinus'), has yellow bands across the narrow green leaves, and dainty plumes of silky white flowers flushed red or purple.

Some silver grasses grow up to 3m/10ft tall; zebra grass only reaches about 1.2m/4ft. They are herbaceous, but the dead foliage can be left on the plant to provide winter interest, and when cut back in spring the plants grow with astonishing speed.

Bamboos are a kind of giant

grass, with hollow woody stems. They make fine specimen plants, but need careful choice as some are very invasive, spreading widely by underground rhizomes, and some can also reach 6m/20ft high.

A good choice for the small garden is *Arundinaria (Sinarundinaria) murielae*, which forms clumps of arching yellow-green canes 2.1-3m/7-10ft tall, topped with dark green leaves, and is non-invasive. It is moderately hardy, but it needs to be protected from cold winds. Plant other bamboos in tubs to control the rhizomes, or sever them regularly with a spade.

Herbaceous plants with

Many varieties of spurge are rather small, but larger ones are good architectural plants. The stems of Euphorbia characias wulfenii (right), for instance, can reach 1.2m/4ft. It is a perennial with biennial stems; each bears densely-packed grey-green leaves one year, and masses of yellow-green blooms the following spring.

The finely divided, fresh green, outer fronds of the ostrich fern (Matteuccia struthiopteris, below) are sterile. Darker, fertile inner fronds appear in the summer.

huge leaves are best planted alone, as a feature in a front garden, or to fill an odd corner, though they might find a place at the back of a large border.

Friendly giants

One such is ornamental rhubarb (*Rheum palmatum*), related to ordinary rhubarb but inedible. The great glossy leaves, deeply toothed, can span 90cm/3ft, and form massive clumps. Large spikes of small fluffy pink flowers up to 2.4m/8ft high are produced in early summer. This plant does best in full sun and moist soil.

An equally handsome moisture-loving plant, with umbrella-shaped leaves up to 30cm/1ft across, and creamy white flower plumes, is *Rodgersia podophylla*. The leaves start off bronze, turn green and finish up coppery.

Not so big, but striking in shape and much loved by painters and sculptors, are the leaves of bear's breeches (*Acanthus spinosus*). They are deeply, jaggedly cut, each division tipped with a spine (perhaps the name comes from the idea that only a bear could tolerate them next to the skin!)

GARDEN NOTES

ATTRACTING BIRDS

Several handsome architectural plants produce seed heads that will attract finches and other seed-eaters if left on the plant in winter. Best ones are:
- Sunflower – huge yellow daisy with central boss of seeds; hardy annual.
- Teasel – large oval prickly seed heads; hardy biennial.

and up to 40cm/16in long. The sturdy flower spikes are equally striking, consisting of white and purple tubular blooms protected by leafy spine-tipped

bracts. The plant grows to about 1.2m/4ft high.

As they reproduce by spores, ferns do not flower, and their interest lies solely in their graceful fronds. They are ideal as architectural plants in wild or woodland gardens, where yuccas or pampas grass would look out of place, and are generally ultra-hardy, preferring a moist soil and shade.

Fascinating ferns

Although herbaceous ferns are interesting for most of the year, in spring they slowly unfurl from tightly coiled heads to reveal the full glory of the fresh green, multi-divided fronds. These are followed by fertile fronds, differently

The yucca genus has many members. All have masses of long, sharp, lance-shaped, arching leaves and infrequent, but spectacular, shows of flowers. The only drawback is that some are on the tender side. Y. gloriosa 'Variegata' (above) is hardier than some, and well worth growing for its yellow-edged leaves and huge panicles of pendulous, creamy-white flowers.

The rhubarb genus is another with many spectacular members. Rheum palmatum (left) is typical, forming a spreading clump of massive, lobed leaves and panicles of tiny, off-white, early summer flowers.

shaped and coloured. Some turn bronze in autumn, and the old brown fronds remain attractive in winter.

There is a multitude of fern species, all subtly different. Good tall ones include the native British buckler fern (*Dryopteris*), with delicate, pale green arching fronds, and the ostrich or shuttlecock fern (*Matteuccia*). This is more upright, and named for the way the fronds resemble a vase full of ostrich feathers, which later surround a shuttlecock-shaped circle of shorter, darker, fertile fronds.

The shield fern (*Polystichum*) is less tall and more spreading, with very finely divided fronds growing from a distinctive brown midrib. Perhaps most handsome of all is the royal fern (*Osmunda*), that can grow to 1.8m/6ft tall. Its fertile fronds resemble dried flowers, and in autumn it turns a rich brown.

Golden and Glorious

The colour of the sun, yellow raises the spirits and warms the heart. Golden flowers or foliage allow the gardener to create sunny cheer all year round.

There are few sights more uplifting than a yellow summer border in full sun (above). The addition of white to the planting prevents the mix from being too overpowering and has the effect of making the colours surrounding it more pure. Here, the composition is helped by a patch of low-growing golden nasturtiums in the front corner.

Yellow must surely be the most useful and versatile colour for the garden. Red may be dramatically eye-catching, orange may be hot and wonderfully gaudy, blue and purple may be sombre and tranquil, and green may be restful – all creating splendid effects in their own way – but a garden without yellow plants lacks the invigorating, sunny cheerfulness that this lovely colour provides.

Yet yellow is invaluable in other ways, too. Its clarity and brightness make it an excellent tool for controlling how the eye 'reads' the garden, with its various perspectives and features, and its effect on other colours gives the gardener a magnificent palette of temperatures and moods with which to paint a multitude of different pictures.

Yellow demonstrates this versatility throughout the year. It is the most welcome of colours in the spring, when primroses and massed daffodils provide a hint of things to come. The glorious variety of summer bedding plants presents the greatest opportunity to play with colour, and there are few who fail to appreciate the golden yellows of autumn foliage. Even in winter, the colour can bring cheer to the gloomy, chill days before the welcoming promise of the daffodil is extended once again.

Summer planting

It may seem odd to begin in the summer, but at no other time are the virtues and versa-

Among the best early summer yellows are the profusion of petite pea-shaped flowers provided by the broom *Genista lydia (left)*, which forms a low, dome-shaped shrub or, as here, trails delightfully over and down a wall, and the tall flowers spikes of *Verbascum 'Gainsborough' (right)*.

tility of yellow more apparent than in the blaze of the mid-summer garden. The effects achieved then can be applied to differing degrees through the rest of the year to bring sunny vitality to every month.

Splashes of yellow give eye-catching structure and weight to the summer border. In larger plantings, the 2m/6ft towering spires of *Verbascum olympicum* and the smaller *V.* 'Gainsborough' contrast with the dense, plate-like heads of *Achillea filipendulina* 'Gold

Rudbeckia fulgida is one of several garden flowers commonly known as black-eyed Susan. 'Goldsturm' (above) is a free-flowering perennial whose golden buttery-yellow flowers, each topping a long, straight stem, are equally pleasing in all-yellow beds or, as here, planted with an orange or red single dahlia.

Plate' and the frothy clouds of golden rod (*Solidago* spp.).

Further pools of yellow to set against this spectacular backdrop – or to give similar structure to smaller plantings – are provided by shrubs, perennials and annuals. The daisy-like blooms of *Chrysanthemum* (or *Argyranthemum*) *frutescens* 'Jamaica Primrose', *Anthemis tinctoria* 'E.C. Buxton' and the later flowering rudbeckias introduce a mass of happy faces.

Bushy *Coreopsis verticillata* carries many star-shaped, golden flowers towards the front of the border, where yellow calceolarias and smaller potentillas such as the 20cm/8in high *P. megalantha* mix with violas and the well-named poached-egg flower (*Limnanthes douglasii*).

Using foliage

Consider foliage when planning any border arrangement, using the mix of greens, silver and greys to draw the different elements together into a pleasing display.

Grey foliage tends to accen-

147

tuate the purity and brightness of flowers around it, so include, for example, the finely-cut silvery foliage of *Artemisia arborescens*, which grows to about 1.2m/4ft, and the low-growing woolly grey leaves of lamb's tongue or bunnies' ears (*Stachys byzantina* or *S. lanata*). *Senecio* 'Sunshine' offers the double advantage of silvery-grey young leaves and large clusters of bright yellow daisy-like flowers in summer.

As an alternative, golden foliage continues the yellow theme, adding further touches of glowing colour. The luxuriantly sculptural leaves of the plantain lily (*Hosta* spp.) are widely appreciated, especially for shadier spots. Several varieties have golden variegations in mid-summer, among them *H.* 'Gold Standard' and *H. fortunei* 'Aureo-marginata'.

A sunshine bed

Make the best of very sunny borders and those which enjoy piercing evening rays with bold, hot combinations of colour. Since strong sunlight bleaches colour, the brightest golden yellows have the advantage in such positions. Combined with vibrant reds and oranges, the resulting fiery effect enriches the sun's warmth and emphasizes the glory of the season.

Add blues to the yellow border and an altogether different effect is created. The combination is invigorating and refreshing, and enchantingly cool in the height of summer. Link the contrasting colours with foliage, and add touches of purple and violet to build a richer, slightly warmer picture. Again, save the strongest colours for sunny positions and use paler tints in shadier areas where they will shine all the more clearly for the lack of bleaching rays.

Yellow-flowering trees and shrubs elsewhere in the garden give continuity to the overall scheme. The magnifi-

cent Mount Etna broom (*Genista aetnensis*) carries a profusion of golden-yellow pea-like flowers in mid-summer but is rather large, growing to 6m/20ft or more. *Genista cinerea,* at half the size, is an excellent alternative, or consider the relatively tiny *G. lydia,* at about 45cm/

A really sunny annual bed (above) benefits from a strong show of hot yellows, oranges and reds. A good source of such floral colour are the dahlias, which include dozens of handsome gold and yellow varieties, such as the semi-cactus 'Davenport Pride' (above left).

148

Clematis rehderiana (above right) is at its best in early autumn. The subtle, creamy yellow of its delicate, bell-like flowers – quite unlike the more familiar, showier varieties of clematis – are more like the spring shades of primroses than the burnished golds of autumn.

The shades of yellow provided by variegated foliage can prove as delightful as those found in flowers. Variegated forms of ivy (Hedera helix) make excellent backdrops or make features in their own right. 'Buttercup' (above), given full sun, will produce glossy, creamy-yellow leaves that contrast wonderfully with the textures of old wood and tiles. Hosta 'Sun Power' (left) is particularly valuable because it produces its handsomely-shaped greenish-yellow leaves in shady conditions.

18in, for the rock garden or trailing over a wall.

The rich golden-yellow saucer-shaped blooms of *Fremontodendron californicum* appear in May and often last into August. It's a large, evergreen shrub, wide-spreading and growing to 6m/20ft or more, so needs pruning to keep it under control, but, set against a sunny wall, it brings a taste of Californian sunshine to the garden.

Lovely laburnum

Childhood warnings against the poisonous seeds never seem to lessen our appreciation of the golden chains of flowers that cascade from the branches of a laburnum. Grown over a walkway or arbour, this deciduous spreading tree makes a glorious feature in spring and early summer.

For soft yellow foliage throughout the summer months, the graceful Japanese maple *Acer japonicum* 'Aureum' is unbeatable. Very slow-growing, it won't achieve its mature height of about 6m/20ft for many years, and this, together with its bushy form and beautiful fan-shaped leaves, makes it ideal for smaller gardens.

Many of the summer golds and yellows continue to bring warmth and cheer to the shor-

EVERGREEN GOLD

The variegated or golden foliage of evergreen species is invaluable for year-round splashes of gold or yellow, bridging the seasons and linking floral colour, and especially useful in winter when the garden can look cold and bare.

A small shrub, *Euonymus fortunei* 'Emerald 'n' Gold' gives a spectacular show of bright green edged generously with gleaming yellow. *Aucuba japonica* 'Crotonifolia', growing to about 2.1m/7ft, has large, glossy, dark green leaves which are heavily mottled with yellow, and the larger *Elaeagnus pungens* 'Maculata' bears dark green leaves with large central patches of deep yellow.

The ivies *Hedera helix* 'Goldheart' and 'Buttercup' provide gorgeous golden colour for scrambling over walls ('Buttercup' does so only in sun), while the box honeysuckle *Lonicera nitida* 'Baggesen's Gold' may be trimmed into neat hedging.

For bright yellow foliage, the Mexican orange blossom (*Choisya ternata* 'Sundance') is surely unbeatable. On a much smaller scale, *Saxifraga moschata* 'Cloth of Gold' is aptly named for the rock garden. When seeking plants with golden foliage colour look for the word 'aurea' (meaning 'golden') which is often used in the plants varietal name.

tening days of autumn. In the borders, the chrysanthemums and dahlias provide an enormous range of shape and colour, the yellows including the single pale daisy-like flowers of *Chrysanthemum* 'Mary Stoker' and the bright spiky balls of *Dahlia* 'Davenport Sunlight'.

Corydalis lutea has tiny tubular yellow flowers which may persist from late autumn. The flowers are carried over delicate, fern-like evergreen foliage, brightening nooks and crannies in walls and steps. A late-flowering clematis – *C. rehderiana* with primrose-yellow bells, or *C. tangutica* with its yellow lanterns – provides a cheerful backdrop or highlights favourite garden features and corners.

These yellows, mixed with hot oranges and reds, enrich the spectacle created by the fiery colours of autumn foliage. The leaves of the Chinese witch hazel (*Hamamelis mollis*) and the Japanese maple *Acer palmatum* 'Senkaki' are particularly notable for their shimmering yellow hues.

Winter sunshine

Foliage is especially important as autumn cools into winter. The lovely rich colouring of slow-growing conifers and dwarf pines such as *Thuja occidentalis* 'Rheingold' and the spreading *Pinus mugo* 'Ophir' provide golden structure.

Alyssum saxatile (above) richly deserves its common name, gold dust. Some catalogues may refer to this plant as **Aurinia saxatilis**.

THE HERB GARDEN

In summer, the herb garden seen from a distance can recede into a blur of pinks and purples, especially where limited space has restricted choice to the commonly grown thymes, mints and so on.

It's well worth finding room for a few yellow-flowering herbs, or adding species with variegated foliage, to give this useful planting a greater, more cheerful presence within the garden as a whole.

Add tall fennel (*Foeniculum vulgare*) and dill (*Anethum graveolens*), which have spreading clusters of yellow flowers on erect stems, the sunny daisies of yellow ox-eye chamomile (*Anthemis tinctoria*) or the delightful, tiny, glowing pompons of cotton lavender (*Santolina chamaecyparissus*) with its delightful silver-grey foliage.

Use gold and variegated foliage varieties for longer-lasting patches of colour: try golden sage (*Salvia officinalis* 'Icterina'), ginger mint (*Mentha × gentilis*), the thyme 'Doone Valley' and the golden lemon thyme (*Thymus × citriodorus* 'Bertram Anderson'). Golden lemon balm (*Melissa officinalis* 'Aurea') and golden marjoram (*Origanum onites* 'Aureum') provide excellent golden foliage for edging.

Turning leaves are one of the best sources of yellow in the autumn, and few trees put on such a purely yellow display as the maple variety Acer palmatum *'Senkaki' (above).*

Yellow also has its place in the herb garden; many herbs have golden leaves. Variegated lemon balm (Melissa officinalis *'Aurea') is an excellent example (above right).*

The pale yellow of primroses is brought out by interplanting them with blue bulbs such as hyacinth (left). Here, Hyacinthus *'Ostara' accompanies* Primula *'Crescendo Lemon Yellow'.*

Several trees and shrubs produce an attractive show of yellow flowers in late winter, among them the spidery, fragrant inflorescences of witch hazel and the clusters of tiny feathery pompons of early-flowering acacias. *Mahonia japonica,* too, casts out long spreading sprays of fragrant yellow flowers from autumn to spring above its distinctive spiny foliage.

The winter flowering jasmine (*Jasminum nudiflorum*) gives a welcome display of bright yellow flowers on leafless shoots trained against a wall or, perhaps, cascading down a bank. Its colour may be echoed in a profusion of sunny yellow winter aconites (*Eranthis hyemalis*), or the shallow golden cups of *Adonis amurensis,* which smile out from beneath shrubs and trees and from border edges.

As yellow crocuses and narcissi in a multitude of sunny shades take over from winter aconites, we know that spring has arrived.

Yellow is, indeed, the colour most evocative of spring, but especially so when in partnership with blue, echoing the much-loved visions of primroses and bluebells.

In the garden, the graceful shrubs of *Forsythia suspensa,* with pale yellow flowers, and Jews's mallow (*Kerria japonica*), which bears buttercup-yellow blooms, are perfect when they are underplanted with Spanish bluebells (*Endymion hispanicus*).

Joys of spring

Among a vast array of yellow spring plants, one of the best, and earliest flowering, is the climbing banksian rose (*Rosa banksiae* 'Lutea') with its sprays of buttery blooms. Use this in combination with the ever-popular *Alyssum saxatile,* known appropriately as gold dust, to herald the coming of summer.

All White

Using white-flowered plants and those with creamy white or silver foliage in your garden give it a feeling of extra space and a sense of calm.

White flowers and silvery foliage can be used in many ways to produce glistening and gleaming effects. During the day, white provides a strong focus; as the sun surrenders to the evening twilight, white and silver accents gleam like bright moonlight.

Strictly speaking, white is neither a colour nor the absence of colour. In fact, it is all the colours of the spectrum present at the same time. As a result, it enhances and enlivens those colours with which it is combined.

White flowers will, by contrast, deepen the dominant colour of a bed or border. They also act to defuse and cool down hot colours that might be too brash to get on well together. Even a narrow drift of white between the colours will put a surprising amount of space between two inharmonious or harsh colours.

Plants with grey and silver foliage also work well as buffers between clashing colours. When combined with white flowers, they add to the shimmering effect.

White drifts

The effect of white is best seen if a white area is enclosed or otherwise separated from the rest of the garden. Make the entrance to a white garden as narrow as possible. When you step through it, you will be instantly struck by the sense of space created by the combination of white and green.

Of course, few gardens have space for an enclosed garden of any size. Fortunately, white

A pure white garden is perhaps beyond the scope of most people, but there is no denying the effect of white flowers against green foliage (above). Here, the pure white rose, Rosa 'Iceberg', is planted with white valerian.

Foliage plants also contribute to an overall 'white' look. Artemisia ludoviciana albula (right) has soft, grey, woolly leaves which complement the plumes of dainty summer flowers.

The tiny, white double flowers of Gypsophila paniculata dissolve into a cloud when seen from even a short distance (far right). Here, it is planted with the pale, wispy, lavender-coloured flowers of nepeta.

can also be used to good effect in borders of mixed hues, creating a deeper colour range and acting as a buffer between strong colours.

Many plants suit this role. The flowers of a white achillea such as *A. ptarmica* 'The Pearl' stand so strongly apart from its foliage that you hardly notice it. It grows to 75cm/2½ft and spreads quickly to form clumps. On a summer evening, its numerous small white flowers dance like tiny stars through the garden.

Another favourite is the small-flowered perennial gypsophila (*G. paniculata* 'Bristol Fairy'). Once again, the flowers dominate by sheer force of numbers, despite the small size of the blooms.

Everlasting pearl (*Anaphalis margaritacea*) and the white variety of rose campion (*Lychnis coronaria* 'Alba') are useful for the middle and front of a border. Both have soft, velvety-textured silver leaves and white heads of attractive summer flowers.

For the back of a border, choose a white foxglove (*Digitalis purpurea* 'Alba'). It may be difficult to buy as a plant, but seed is available and its tall, elegant spires of pure white flowers make a delightful contribution to a drift of white in the border.

Edges

White's ability to separate areas of colour and interest makes it a particularly useful colour at the edges of a bed or a border, where low-growing white or silver plants really

The flowers of **Achillea** ptarmica *'The Pearl' – also known as 'Boule de Neige' – (above) make up in numbers what they lack in size.*

RECOMMENDED VARIETIES

Plant	Description	Season
Perennials		
Achillea ptarmica 'The Pearl'	Clusters of white flowers. Spreads quickly	Summer
Everlasting pearl (*Anaphalis margaritacea*)	Silver foliage, clusters of white flowers	Late summer
Artemisia (*Artemisia ludoviciana albula*)	Silver, aromatic leaves. Grey-white flowers.	Summer
Dianthus 'Mrs Sinkins'	Old-fashioned pink with white flowers and silver foliage.	Spring/ Summer
Foxglove (*Digitalis purpurea* 'Alba')	Short-lived perennials with tubular white flowers.	Summer
Gypsophila paniculata 'Bristol Fairy'	Small, double white flowers	Summer
Lychnis coronaria 'Alba'	Silver stems and leaves; white flowers	Mid-late summer
*Senecio maritima (*syn. *Cineraria maritima*) 'Silver Dust' & 'Cirrhus'	Silver foliage; half-hardy.	All year
Annuals		
Sweet alyssum (*Alyssum maritima* 'Little Dorrit')	Greyish leaves, small, white, scented flowers.	Summer to autumn
Matthiola 'Giant Imperial'	Greyish leaves, creamy white scented flowers	Spring/ summer

come into their own.

For edging beds with silver, the traditional choice is senecio (*Senecio maritima*), with its deeply-cut, soft-textured leaves. Both 'Silver Dust' and 'Cirrhus' are useful contrast plants though, because of its low-growing habit, 'Silver Dust' is more often used as an edging or bedding plant.

Artemisias provide silver foliage for the middle and back of the border. *Artemisia ludoviciana albula* offers silver leaves and tiny, grey-white flowers in summer. It grows to about 1.2m/4ft in height, flopping in a lax way as it spreads, but this increases its usefulness as a barrier plant.

Silver carpets
One of the most useful silver foliage plants is *Helichrysum petiolare*. Its soft-textured, silvery-white leaves are carried on arching stems that trail attractively over the edges when planted in a container. It is also used as an edging plant in a mixed border or as mound-forming ground cover. The foliage is complemented by small, creamy flowers in summer.

Snow-in-summer (*Cerastium tomentosum*) combines greyish leaves with small white flowers to make a dense ground cover; it will smother a dry, sunny bank with a flush of silver and white. It is also a good rockery plant and tumbles attractively over the sides

White is a good background, throwing colours forward (above). Here, the full blooms of Rosa *'Iceberg' and the pendent panicles of Russian vine* (Polygonum baldschuanicum) *set off a bed of dahlias.*

Among the several paradoxically white varieties of pink, Dianthus *'Mrs Sinkins' (far left) stands out for purity of colour.*

Varieties of Hydrangea paniculata *(left) have white flower-heads that are conical in shape rather than the more familiar dome shape.*

Helichrysum petiolare, *also known as* H. petiolatum, *forms mounds of grey-green foliage from which spring pale cream summer flower-heads. It is best used in a container, as here, or as edging for a border.*

of tall terracotta containers. One of its most useful roles is as ground cover at the base of an evergreen conifer hedge.

Rose choice
White roses are probably the most popular plants of any white feature in a garden. There are many pure whites, but the best choice is perhaps *Rosa* 'Iceberg'. It produces clusters of cupped, double flowers, and can be used as a bush rose or, in its climbing form, against a trellis or up a pillar. It flowers from summer through to autumn.

Many white-flowered shrubs will provide waves of blooms in season, but, once flowering is over, their green foliage will dominate. Hydrangeas, viburnum, lilac and the butterfly bush (*Buddleia davidii*) all have lovely white forms that will make a bold and attractive show in season.

The mock orange (*Philadelphus* spp.) is popular for its densely packed white flowers, redolent of orange blossom, which are borne on graceful arching stems against glossy foliage; try planting *P.* 'Belle Etoile' or, for double flowers, *P.* 'Boule d'Argent'.

Many species of daisy bush have a happy combination of white flowers and silver foliage. They suit a mixed border or can be used as white accents against a shed or near the house. Both *Olearia virgata* – which can grow to 6m/20ft

– and the more contained *O. mollis* (1m/3ft) have dense heads of white, daisy-like flowers that are set off well by their attractive silvery-grey or grey-green leaves.

Small shrubs
With its yellow-centred, white trumpet flowers and silvery-green leaves, *Convolvulus cneorum* is a perfect choice as a small specimen shrub. Frost-hardy, and growing to a height and spread of 1m/3ft, it suits a sunny, well-drained, mixed shrub and perennial border. It will also make an attractive year-round buffer in your colour scheme.

Smaller and equally well-suited to a dry, sunny site is *Dorycnium hirsutum*, a bushy

A WHITE BULB GARDEN

You can enjoy a succession of white flowers from bulbous plants through the year, beginning with the early spring crocus, *Crocus sieberi* 'Bowles' White' or 'Alba'. Other spring bulbs, such as tulips, narcissus, grape hyacinth and of course snowdrops all come in white and creamy forms. The spring star flower (*Ipheion uniflorum*) is usually blue, but a white variety will add style and charm.

In summer, lilies – including the Madonna lily – gladioli and camassia bring unusual shapes and flower forms to the bulb garden (right), followed by the appearance of white autumn crocus (*Colchicum speciosum* 'Album'). Winter white comes from varieties of *Cyclamen coum*.

The large (12cm/5in across) flowers of Clematis 'Henryi' (above left) provide bold areas of well-defined white at the height of summer.

Dorycnium hirsutum (right) is a low-growing (60cm/24in) shrub whose silver-edged leaves make it a good choice for a white garden; the pink flush on the flower buds gives way as they open to a pure white flower.

Silver plants make a wonderful background foil for pink or red flowers, deepening the red tones. Use artemisias behind and around pink roses, or next to penstemons or diascia (above).

The tortuous branches of the woody climber Wisteria floribunda 'Alba' provide interest even in the winter months, when the pale green leaves have gone, but the plant is in its full glory in early summer (above), when long, white racemes of sweetly-scented white flowers drip from its gracefully arching branches.

plant with silky-textured silver-grey leaves. In summer, its pinkish-white buds open to white, pea-like flowers.

White climbers

White-flowered climbing plants grown on trellis extensions above boundary walls or against the back wall of the house offer a sense of extra space and height. Many have the added attraction of fragrant flowers.

White wisteria (*Wisteria sinensis* 'Alba') grows at least 6m/20ft on each spreading stem. Its vanilla-scented pea-like flowers hang in long trails in early summer. For a pergola, choose white Japanese wisteria (*W. floribunda* 'Alba').

Several clematis provide seasonal successions of white flowers to grace your patio walls. In a protected, sunny position, grow the evergreen white clematis (*C. armandii*), with scented early spring flowers. For mid-season white use *Clematis* 'Henryi' and for late summer flowers choose *Clematis flammula*.

Standing alone

Well-shaped specimen trees or shrubs make very useful large white accents in a garden. If you have the space for a good-sized tree, the white-flowered cherry (*Prunus avium* 'Plena') offers clouds of double white flowers all through the spring. It can reach up to 12m/40ft.

Smaller, but equally generous with their spring flowers, are two other cherries, *P.* 'Mount Fuji' and *P.* 'Tai Haku'. They form round heads and can reach 8m/24ft.

One of the most unusual white-flowering trees is a dogwood (*Cornus controversa* 'Variegata') known as the wedding cake tree because of its tiered branches. At its mature height of 8m/24ft it makes a very full crown. However, the combination of delicate, white summer flowers and creamy white variegated leaves give it a light and airy appearance.

Silver threads

For a similar effect in silvery-grey, use weeping pear (*Pyrus salicifolia* 'Pendula'). In full sun, it grows to a height and spread of up to 10m/30ft, half that in a small garden. It has small white spring flowers and weeping branches that sweep the ground, making an informal hedge-like mound.

Variegated, silver-edged forms of holly also produce sparkling effects, especially when they are caught by rays of winter sunlight. *Ilex aquifolium* 'Silver Queen', for example, is, despite its name, a male plant, so will not bear red berries to detract from your garden's silvery theme.

Bare Branches

Autumn is usually the end for deciduous trees and shrubs, but some continue to please the eye with the shape, colour and texture of their stems and branches.

For most of the year, the framework of trees and shrubs is invisible beneath the foliage. Any charms it may possess remain hidden until the autumn. Once the leaves have followed the flowers into memory, plants with attractive bark and brightly coloured or twisting stems come into their own, extending garden interest through the winter months.

Such plants provide a strong, sometimes stark, focus in the winter garden, especially when they are caught by stray rays of angled sunlight.

Willows

Golden and weeping willows are large trees, suitable only for a parkland or riverside setting. However, there are many attractively coloured and unusually shaped willows that can be grown in more modest surroundings.

Salix alba 'Britzensis', for instance, has bright, glowing red stems. You can control its vigour and ensure good, new coloured shoots by cutting it back to ground level in spring, a procedure known as stooling.

Another way of pruning this willow is pollarding; leave the young tree until it has reached a height of 1.2m/4ft. At this stage, cut all side and top growth back to the trunk. This results in a bristling head of new, vigorous straight shoots.

The violet willow (*Salix daphnoides*) also responds well to drastic pruning, producing a flush of new shoots covered with a purplish bloom.

In spring the stems are studded with large rosy buds that open to reveal fluffy catkins.

Ideal for a small garden is *Salix hastata* 'Wehrhahnii', with its upright, bushy growing habit and purple-coloured new stems. As an added winter attraction, it produces catkins that sparkle a lovely silver-grey in the sunlight.

Willows grow well in most soils and only fail to do well in very dry situations. To see them at their best, you should grow them in a sunny spot and prune them hard every year in early spring.

Some trees have forms with dramatically twisted and con-

torted trunk and branches. They are best appreciated when they are seen against a background of solid colour or a clear winter sky.

Although they are an acquired taste – the trees can look diseased to those not familiar with them – they make quite an impact in a small garden. Both corkscrew willow (*Salix matsudana* 'Tortuosa') and contorted hazel (*Corylus avellana* 'Contorta') can be kept to a suitably reasonable height and spread.

Splendid dogwoods

Shrubs in the dogwood genus (*Cornus* spp.) are primarily grown for their vivid stems in a variety of bright colours.

Red-barked dogwood (*C. alba* 'Sibirica') produces gleaming red stems, while those of *C. stolonifera* 'Flaviramea' are greeny-yellow. In

RECOMMENDED PLANTS

Plant	Notes	Interest
Willow		
Salix alba 'Britzensis'	cut back in spring	bright red-orange shoots
S. daphnoides	cut back in spring	purple-white bloom on new shoots
S. hastata 'Wehrhahnii'	1.5m/5ft tall bush	purple shoots/silver catkins
S. matsudana 'Tortuosa'	cut back to keep in bounds	twisted stems
Hazel		
Corylus avellana 'Contorta'	6m/20ft	twisted stems, pale yellow catkins
Dogwoods		
Cornus alba 'Sibirica'	2.4m/8ft cut back in spring	red stems
C. stolonifera 'Flaviramea'	2m/6ft cut back in spring	greeny-yellow stems
C. alba 'Kesselringii'	2.4/8ft cut back in spring	purple/black stems
C. sanguinea 'Winter Flame' (syn. 'Winter Beauty')	2.4m/8ft cut back in spring	flame orange stems
Birch		
Betula papyrifera	Large tree	white papery bark
B. pendula	Large tree	silvery bark
B. utilis jacquemontii	15m/50ft	pure white peeling bark
Maple		
Acer griseum	10m/33ft	brown-orange peeling bark
A. grosseri	10m/33ft	black and white striped
A. palmatum 'Senkaki'	6m/20ft	pink shoots
Flowering cherries		
Prunus serrula	15m/50ft	peeling mahogany bark
Prunus incisa 'Kojo-no-mai'	90-120cm/3-4ft	twiggy shape, flowers on bare stem
Bare stems and flowers		
Witch hazel spp.	4m/12ft	russet/yellow flowers on bare stems
Winter flowering jasmine (*Jasminum nudiflorum*)	3m/10ft climber	yellow flowers on green stems
Viburnum (*Viburnum* × *bodnantense* 'Dawn')	3m/10ft	reddish-brown stems and pink flowers
Daphne (*Daphne mezereum*)	1.5m/5ft	dark stems with deep pink flowers
Stachyurus praecox	3m/10ft	wine red stems/yellow flowers
Corylopsis pauciflora	3m/10ft	dark stems/yellow flowers in spring

When its golden leaves have fallen, **Acer pensylvanicum 'Erythrocladum'** *produces bright pink shoots (far left).*

The tortuous twigs of contorted hazel drip with yellow catkins in late winter (top).

Dogwood stems are a prime source of winter colour. Those of **Cornus stolonifera 'Flaviramea' (left) are a brilliant greeny-yellow.**

sharp contrast, *Cornus alba* 'Kesselringii' has stems which are dark purple, almost black. All three of these plants look attractive in single colour groups or grown with each other in mixed groupings.

Plant *Helleborus foetidus*, which has pale green winter flowers, in front of your dogwood, and see that the background foliage colour is a suitable foil for these bright plants; dark evergreens or golden conifers usually make the best backdrops.

A really dazzling dogwood is *C. sanguinea* 'Winter Flame', also known as 'Winter Beauty', whose autumn leaves and winter stems live up to its varietal names. Cut it back in spring and the first flush of new shoots will start to grow ready for next winter's show.

For best effect, dogwoods should be grown in full sun in well-drained soil. They are,

159

PATIO CHERRY

For an all-year colour show on a patio, grow the dwarf form of Fuji cherry (*Prunus incisa* 'Kojo-no-mai'). In winter it offers a mass of twisting, delicate twigs that make an unusual but attractive shape.

In spring, the black twigs produce brown buds that turn red before bursting into blossom. In autumn, its leaves put on a dramatic display, changing from brown to orange and crimson before falling to unmask their twiggy framework.

Fuji cherry grows well in tubs given a position in full sun, and reaches 90-120cm/3-4ft.

however, fairly tolerant of moist soils.

Most birch trees will grow too large for the small garden, but if you need a light screening plant at the end of a long, narrow plot, they certainly fit the bill. A mature example of the quick-growing common silver birch (*Betula pendula*) has silvery bark with dark markings; two or three together make an attractive feature.

Birch bark

Other members of the genus have more exotic bark. Canoe or paper birch (*B. papyrifera*) is suitable for only the largest of gardens, but shares its most decorative characteristic with the more manageable, pure white Himalayan birch (*B.*

SITING TREES

If you decide to plant one of the medium to large trees for their ornamental bark avoid siting them too near your own or your neighbour's foundations. Tree roots can cause damage and if they are too near the house the developing crowns will eventually block out valuable light.

utilis jacquemontii). In both these trees the bark peels and curls away from the trunk, hanging from it in paper-thin streamers that glow delightfully when struck by shafts of afternoon sunlight.

Birches grow best in moist, well-drained soils in full sun.

Maples are grown for their autumn colour, but for some the show is not over when the last leaf has fallen. One of the best for a smaller garden – it grows to an eventual height of 10m/30ft, so be sure it has room to develop – is the paperbark maple (*Acer griseum*).

As it matures, its orangebrown bark begins to peel and curl, leaving random light brown patches. In the warm light of the late evening sun, this creates a truly beautiful dappled effect.

Sometimes the colour, rather than the texture of the bark is remarkable. One of the snake-bark maples, *A. grosseri*, with black and white stripes on its trunk and branches, offers an attractive architectural focus in winter,

while the coral-bark maple (*A. palmatum* 'Senkaki') is a useful shrub or small tree for the back of a mixed border planting. Its bright pink young shoots make a colourful contribution in the winter, while it puts on a foliage display of great variety through the rest of the year. It is slow growing, but eventually reaches a height of 6m/20ft.

All maples grow well in well-drained, neutral or slightly acid soil. They require full sun.

Flowering stems

Many plants bear flowers in the early spring, before their leaves open, providing an uncluttered, pure display of jewel-like colour along the bare stems and branches. This is true, for instance, of ornamental cherries. In some species of cherry, the trunk and branches have splendid added attractions of their own.

Prunus serrula, for instance, has shiny red to mahogany-coloured bark that, like that of the paper birch, peels away in curling streamers that con-

The upright stems of the bushy shrub willow Salix hastata 'Wehrhanii' are purple when new, turning yellow with age. The plant's main glory, though, is its silvery catkins, which appear before the leaves in early spring (left).

Several trees have peeling bark, but few are so spectacular as the ornamental cherry Prunus serrula (right). The tattered remnants of old bark that continue to cling on are barely noticeable alongside the rich coppery-red sheen of the new.

Like most of the maples, Acer palmatum 'Senkaki' has attractive, brightly-coloured autumn leaves. In this variety, though, the interest is sustained through the winter months by its coral-pink new shoots, that look particularly beautiful when they are covered with a light dusting of frost (left).

P ROJECT

A DOGWOOD GROUP

Plant dogwoods in groups of three, allowing each plant sufficient space to spread. They need approximately 1 sq. m/1 sq. yd. each and will eventually grow to overlap each other's space.

Underplant the bed with a variegated creeping ivy, such as Hedera helix 'Glacier' to provide the thin colourful dogwood stems with an anchor.

Site the dogwood bed so that it can be seen against a strongly-coloured evergreen backdrop.

Plant fresh green winter-flowering hellebores (Helleborus foetidus) in front of the dogwoods.

TREE CARE

Until they are well established trees and shrubs need regular watering and mulching in spring with organic matter. Keep competing grasses away from their bases and hand weed to prevent root damage.

Many trees respond to light pruning, but check your trees' special needs first.

Pink is a rare colour in the late winter garden, but **Daphne mezereum** *(below) provides it in great quantity. Its clusters of extremely fragrant four-lobed flowers hug the branches through into early spring, when they are succeeded by bright red fruits.*

trast prettily with the new bark below, which gleams as if it were polished.

One of the newer flowering cherries is a dwarf form of the Fuji cherry (*Prunus incisa* 'Kojo-no-mai'), which makes an attractive plant for a patio tub, growing to 90-120cm/3-4ft. When the leaves are gone, its twiggy form and tortuous branches maintain interest, carrying buds that turn to crimson before bursting into bloom in spring.

Winter warmth

Witch hazels carry their wispy, warm-coloured flowers on bare winter stems, as does the climbing winter-flowering jasmine (*Jasminum nudiflorum*). The fragrant pink blooms of the winter-flowering viburnum, *Viburnum × bodnantense* 'Dawn', are borne on reddish-brown stems.

More specialized, but well worth seeking out, are two very attractive spring-

flowering plants that suit deep mixed borders. *Stachyurus praecox* holds its fragrant yellow flowers along trails that hang from thin, wine-red stems. It grows to 3m/10ft tall. The bushy *Corylopsis pauciflora* also has yellow flowers. They are carried on stems so thin that they disappear at a distance; the flowers appear to be hanging in the air like a shower of golden raindrops.

Bare stems, textured bark and twisted twigs often look their best if plants are grouped together to make a feature. Some need to be viewed against the sky or the contrasting colour of an evergreen's foliage.

Groups of dogwoods look dramatic when underplanted with variegated creeping ivies. The soft foliage of birch groups can be anchored by underplanting the trees with spring bulbs to attract your eye as the birchs' leaves begin to appear in early spring.

PERFECT PARTNERS

Birches are very much trees of open woodland, occurring in clearings and copses rather than in the heart of the forest. By underplanting them with spring bulbs, you can recreate the feel of a sylvan glade.

Ornamental Fruits

Most people think of flowers and foliage when planning an ornamental garden, but many plants earn their place with decorative, if inedible, fruit.

Trees such as apples, pears and cherries, and bushes such as currants and gooseberries, which are grown primarily for their edible fruit, can always find their place in an ornamental garden.

Many other plants produce fruits that – at least in their raw forms – are inedible to us because they are too sour, too hard or simply too distasteful for our palates. However, this is no reason for disregarding them when it comes to planning your garden.

Trees such as crab apple, quince and medlar all produce large, shapely, colourful fruits, as does the unusual and striking strawberry tree.

The fat fruits – hips – of several roses also offer autumn and winter colour, while there are several wild plants that will make up a hedge offering attractive flowers in spring and shining autumn fruits. These include the blue-black fruits of the blackthorn and the sloe, the sour, plum-like bullace, and hawthorn, with its bright red, lantern-like haws. Not only will they make a good boundary but they will also attract a host of birds to your garden to feast at a time when food is scarce.

Climbers such as passion flower (*Passiflora caerulea*) and ornamental gourds also have unusual fruits.

Crab apples

Crab apples (*Malus* spp.) are a popular choice for gardens, providing interest in spring

Crab apples have the same range of greens, yellows and reds as other apples. This one is 'John Downie'.

PRUNING

Most ornamental fruit trees simply need a winter cut back of any dead or damaged branches. Quinces need to be pruned so that a good shaped tree develops. For the first few years, cut back leading shoots to half their previous summer growth.

with their pretty flowers. Once the flowers fall, the miniature apple-like fruits begin to develop. When mature they glow like festive tree ornaments, brightening the garden in autumn and providing the birds with a late feast in winter.

There are several species and varieties of flowering crab apples whose flower, foliage and fruits vary in colour. For white flowers in spring, followed by tightly packed groups of golden fruit, choose *Malus* 'Golden Hornet'. It can grow to 10m/30ft but its upright shape makes it suitable for most gardens.

M. 'John Downie' has spring flowers which are white with pinkish outer edges. It has a narrow, upright shape and its large, reddish-orange fruits make a delicious jelly.

The Japanese crab apple (*M. floribunda*) has pink flowers that open from deep rose-coloured buds. It forms a mophead shape with arching branches that carry small yellow apples in autumn.

With wine red stems, leaves and flowers, *Malus* 'Lemoinei' offers a strong contrast with

The fruit is not always the only ornamental part of an ornamental fruit tree. All crab apples, for instance, bear spring blossom, though few can put on quite such a show as Malus floribunda (left), whose red buds give way to pale pink blossom. The yellow fruit, though just as abundant, is rather small.

The Japenese medlar or loquat (Eriobotrya japonica) flowers in autumn. Its fruits (right) do not ripen fully until the spring, and can be damaged by a succession of winter frosts.

The pear-like fruit of the quince tree (Cydonia oblonga) has an enticing fragrance to go with its pleasing shape. This variety is 'Champion' (below right).

The medlar puts on its best show in autumn, when the fruits – green at first, then darkening and hardening – nestle among beautifully tinted leaves (below).

WINDBREAK APPLES

If you need to create a windbreak at the end of your garden, choose a crab apple tree to do the job.

Upright and compact in their growth, they will soon provide a screen to filter and decrease wind.

terest all year round. In spring medlars bloom with large, cup-shaped, pink-tinged white flowers. In autumn, the leaves turn russet and bronze and the fruits are rusty-brown. Although they can be eaten when soft and half-rotten after a frost, they are usually grown for ornament.

The Japanese medlar (*Eriobotrya japonica*) is an evergreen that needs good warm summers and winter shelter to thrive. It can be grown in a large container on a patio or planted in a sheltered position near south-facing walls. It grows to 8m/25ft and bears fragrant white flower clusters in spring. In autumn, its round green fruits, nestling amongst showy green leaves, deepen in colour and turn yellow as they ripen.

The real quince

If you have space to grow it, a real quince tree (*Cydonia oblonga*) will provide an interesting shape, flowers and large, pear-shaped fruits that you can cook with apples for pies or use for jellies.

Quince trees grow to about 5m/15ft and do well in moist but otherwise ordinary garden soil, in a sunny position. In autumn, quince foliage becomes a glowing yellow. The fruits should be picked before the first frosts spoil them.

Ornamental quince

If space is at a premium, grow the thorny, spring-flowering shrub, flowering quince (*Chaenomeles speciosa*), or japonica (*C. japonica*). Both can

pale-flowered crab apples. Its fruits maintain the purple to burgundy colour scheme when they appear in autumn.

For the very small garden, choose a weeping form; *Malus* 'Sun Rival' can be pruned in summer to keep it compact.

Medlar — an old fruit

The medlar (*Mespilus germanica*) is a tree that has a long history in gardens, offering in-

be used to form hedges, to spread against a wall or as shrubs in a mixed border.

Their spring flowers can be white, deep red, salmony-orange or pink, and are followed by a profusion of yellowy-green round fruits.

The fruits look attractive on the plants in late summer as they mature and by autumn are very decorative. Pick them once they start to fall in autumn winds and use them for pies and jellies as you would real, tree quince fruit.

Strawberries on trees
The strawberry tree (*Arbutus unedo*) grows as a small spreading tree or as a bushy shrub. It carries its small bell-like white flowers in autumn at the same time as its fruits.

At first glance the fruits resemble strawberries, hence the plant's common name. On closer examination, you will see the red fruits have a knobbly hard skin, and look more like the oriental lychee fruit.

Fruits of the rose
The delightful fragrant blooms of roses last for a relatively short season. Some, however, provide an autumn bonus with their fat, coloured fruits. Rose hips vary in size and colour but all of them make attractive material for autumn berry and foliage displays.

Rosa rugosa 'Frau Dagmar Hartopp', often grown to make a low hedge, has fat red hips that contrast well with its own yellowing autumn foliage. *R. rubrifolia*, with its silvery-pink leaves, shows off clusters of delicate, deep red hips that will brighten a mixed border in autumn.

The red-flowered *Rosa moyesii* 'Geranium' has unusual, flask-shaped, orange hips which glow brightly through the autumn months and are 3cm/1in long.

The vigorous climbing rose *R. filipes* 'Kiftsgate' offers autumn jewels in the shape of glowing clusters of small, bright red, pea-like hips.

Wild fruits
If you are starting a garden from scratch, and are able to choose an indigenous, wildlife-attracting hedge, you will also be able to enjoy some of nature's loveliest wild fruits when autumn arrives.

Sloes (*Prunus spinosa*), with their flush of white spring blossom, provide beautiful blue fruit in autumn. Bitter to taste, they can be used in hedgerow jams and jellies and to make country wines.

Bullace (*Prunus institia*) provides arching sprays of plummy, purple or yellow fruit while wild hawthorn (*Crataegus monogyna*) provides clus-

The hard, knobbly fruits of the strawberry tree (Arbutus unedo, above) ripen at the same time as the following year's white flowers appear.

The sloe (Prunus spinosa) bears bluish, plum-like bitter fruit (top right).

The common elder (Sambucus nigra) is rarely welcomed into a garden, but its delicately perfumed flower clusters – used to flavour wines and cordials – and its purple-black berry fruits (mid right), themselves the basis of distinctive wines and jellies, are some consolation for its invasive habits.

All roses have hips, but those of Rosa moyesii 'Geranium' (right) are larger and longer than most.

GARDEN NOTES

TENDER PASSION

Passion flowers are cut back by frost in winter but new growth reappears from the base in spring.

For best results, grow passion flower against a south or west-facing wall, where it benefits from maximum sunshine and reflected warmth. It needs support for its tendrils to twine around.

ters of bell-shaped red fruits.

In most gardens the highly vigorous elder tree (*Sambucus niger*) is an unwanted guest, but it has abundant clusters of attractive berries that provide food for wild birds or tasty jams and jellies.

For extra ornamental value, choose the purple elder (*S. n.* 'Guincho Purple'). Its foliage gradually darkens to a rich purple and its fruits are wine-red to purple. In spring it is particularly lovely, as its deep pink buds open to reveal white flowers. Grow it as a specimen shrub against a lighter foliage background to enhance its graceful arching stems.

Climbing fruits

Grape vines are popular choices to provide edible and ornamental fruit in conservatories and greenhouses, but you can be adventurous with several other climbing plants that offer unusual fruits.

Passion flower (*Passiflora caerulea*) produces its complex flowers through the summer into the autumn. From the flowers, large, rounded, green fruits develop, which turn yellow to orange as they mature. They are edible and can be used to make jams and jellies.

Ornamental gourds (*Cucurbita pepo*) will give you coloured fruits that make excellent indoor decorations. Sow seed in spring under glass in gentle heat. When all danger of frost is over, set the plants into a sunny position. Support them with netting or string tied between canes. As they scramble up, they will flower and produce unusually shaped and variously coloured gourds.

Ornamental gourds are not edible. Simply enjoy them arranged in baskets or bowls as autumn and winter decoration. Pick them when ripe and allow them to dry and harden before applying a coat of varnish to hold the colour.

PERFECT COMPANIONS

Many ornamental fruit trees are deciduous, losing their leaves in autumn, with the fruits staying until either weather or birds have finished them off.

Underplant the trees with common ivy to keep some evergreen interest through the winter. An underplanting of bulbs too, will brighten their winter look.

Theme and Variations

Variegated foliage – green leaves splashed, spotted, striped or edged with contrasting colours – brings exciting extra dimensions to all parts of the garden.

Garden plants which combine beauty with ease of growth and hardiness soon become popular. But this can mean that everyone in your neighbourhood has the same things in their garden!

One way to ring the changes is to choose varieties of common plants whose leaves add extra interest. Plants with attractive foliage are invaluable as vertical or horizontal cover, as edging for a mixed bed or as background to a border; many can also stand alone as specimen plants or be grown together in a foliage garden.

Flowers and foliage

Variegated forms can provide striking contrasts during the flowering season, and add colour and liveliness when there are no blooms. Although they are sometimes slightly less hardy than varieties with solid-coloured leaves, variegated forms are still very reliable if well treated.

GARDEN NOTES

WHY IT HAPPENS

Variegated foliage occurs when some of the plant's cells lose their ability to produce chlorophyll, the green pigment that takes energy from sunlight. The location of these cells accounts for the different patterns – pale edging, blotches and spots all over, or a pale central area.

There are exceptions; some abutilons, for example, owe their spots to a virus infection.

168

Several border perennials have variegated forms, including spring-flowering favourites like London pride *(Saxifrage umbrosa)*, Solomon's seal *(Polygonatum × hybridum)*, and rock cress *(Arabis)*. The lungwort family *(Pulmonaria spp.)* nearly all have prettily spotted leaves, as well as a mass of early flowers resembling blue cowslips.

The huge family of summer-flowering phlox includes *P. paniculata* 'Harlequin', with its violet-purple flowers and cream variegated leaves. The speedwell, prized for its tall, slender spikes of pale blue flowers, also has a variegated form, *Veronica gentianoides* 'Variegata'.

A few pelargoniums (bedding geraniums) have variegated leaves, though their flowers are modest compared

with the more popular varieties. Look for *Pelargonium × peltatum* 'L'Elegante', whose marbled pink and white leaves become deep purple when mature, and *P. crispum* 'Variegatum', whose cream-edged leaves have a delicious, lemony scent. Both have elegant flowers that complement their attractive leaves.

Lacecap hydrangeas, with their pink or blue flower clusters, are even more spectacular when the blooms are augmented by dappled grey-green leaves edged with yellow. Look for *Hydrangea macrophylla* 'Tricolor', 'Variegata' or 'Variegata Mariesii'.

Another large and popular family, the fuchsias, includes *Fuchsia magellanica* – small-flowered but hardier than most – in two variegated forms. 'Variegata' has green leaves edged creamy-yellow and flushed with pink, while 'Versicolor' has rose-tinted young leaves maturing to grey-green marked with creamy-white.

Flowering shrubs

Kerria japonica 'Pleniflora', commonly known as bachelor's buttons, is a common shrub which produces a profusion of double flowers like small yellow pompons. For a refreshing change, look out for *Kerria japonica* 'Variegata', which has single creamy-white flowers and white-edged leaves.

Weigelas, with their vivid pink or red flowers, are frequently used in gardens, not least because they thrive anywhere, including shady spots. For a touch of distinction look for *Weigela florida* 'Variegata', whose creamy-white-edged leaves set off the delicate pink flowers to perfection.

Ground cover

Variegation is a particularly useful feature in ground cover plants, adding colour and pattern to what would otherwise be a mass of undifferentiated green foliage.

Rose of Sharon (*Hypericum calycinum*), for example, is a great ground cover plant as it thrives anywhere, is usually evergreen and produces large, showy yellow flowers; however, its close relative *Hypericum × moseranum* 'Tricolor' is very similar, and has the added bonus of delightful pink-edged leaves.

Similarly, *Pachysandra terminalis*, whose rapidly spreading leaf rosettes make particularly good ground cover under trees, is not very interesting in itself, while the variety 'Variegata' is a much more interesting and brighter plant with green and silver leaves.

For ground cover in shade seek out variegated Siberian

The variegated form of the Siberian bugloss, Brunnera macrophylla 'Variegata' (above), produces sprays of blue flowers, like forget-me-nots, in spring and heart-shaped green and creamy-white leaves which make good ground cover.

Elaeagnus × ebbingii is a hardy evergreen shrub that produces silvery flowers in the autumn. The 'Gilt Edge' variety (below) provides year-round interest with its gold and green foliage, provided it is kept in full sun.

display of scarlet berries.

The common blue-flowered periwinkles, *Vinca major* and *Vinca minor,* are widely used for covering banks and shaded areas with their evergreen leaves. *V. major* 'Variegata' ('Elegantissima') has equally pretty blue flowers, but these are enhanced by yellow-bordered leaves; *V. minor* 'Aureovariegata' has blotched gold and green leaves. Both flourish in shade.

Foliage shrubs

Variegated foliage comes into its own in those plants – usually with insignificant flowers – that are grown specifically for the quality of their leaves. Indeed, it is possible to design an interesting, colourful garden area entirely around specimen shrubs.

Variegated forms of elaeagnus, for instance, give you a handsome evergreen shrub with shiny gold and green leaves. Look for *E. ebbingei* 'Limelight' or 'Gilt Edge'. All widely available forms of *E. pungens* are variegated; 'Maculata' is particularly useful for winter colour.

Similar, and available in a wide range of both gold and silver variegations, is *Euonymus japonicus* (Japanese spindle tree). For something more low-growing look

The leaf rosettes of **Pachysandra terminalis** *'Variegata' (above) make far more interesting evergreen ground cover than the rather dull species. No-one could say* **Weigela florida***, whose funnel-shaped pink flowers appear in late spring, lacks interest, but the 'Variegata' variety (below) makes an attractive shrub throughout the summer.*

bugloss (*Brunnera macrophylla* 'Variegata') as it actually prefers such conditions. It has beautiful, white-splashed, heart-shaped leaves and delicate flowers similar to those of forget-me-nots.

For poor soil, the best ground cover is dead nettle, which can become invasive elsewhere. There are several variegated forms – *Lamium maculatum* 'Beacon Silver' is particularly beautiful, with its pale silvery leaves edged with green.

Vertical cover

The fishbone cotoneaster (*Cotoneaster horizontalis*) is useful for covering both ground and walls; choose 'Variegatus' and get creamy-white-edged leaves that turn pink in autumn, an excellent foil for the cotoneaster's characteristic

171

FIVE HEDGES

Hedges need not be single-coloured masses of foliage. Any of the following will brighten up a barrier.
- Box (*Buxus sempervirens*) 'Aureo-variegata' or 'Elegantissima'. Both are slow-growing.
- Box honeysuckle (*Lonicera nitida*) 'Baggesen's Gold'. Fast-growing.
- Golden privet (*Ligustrum ovalifolium*) 'Aureum'. Fast-growing.
- Hollies (*Ilex* spp.). Many varieties of holly have both gold and silver variegation. They are slow-growing.
- Portugal laurel (*Prunus lusitanica*) 'Variegata'. Fast-growing.

for *E. fortunei* 'Emerald 'n' Gold' or 'Emerald Gaiety'.

A spreading, highly decorative shrub with strikingly large leaves is the angelica tree *(Aralia elata)*. Two variegated forms are available, with either white- or yellow-edged leaves.

For gardens with lime-free soil, *Pieris japonica* is an excellent shrub, with large drooping sprays of white flowers in spring. 'Variegata' has striking cream-edged leaves, pink-tinged when young, but is slow-growing.

Dogwood *(Cornus alba)* is usually grown for the winter colour provided by its red stems, and 'Elegantissima' ('Sibirica Variegata' is similar) complements these later with pale green leaves edged and mottled with white.

Small foliage plants

Two groups of plants give outstanding leaf colour; plantain lilies (hostas) and flame nettles (coleus).

Hostas are ultra-hardy, moisture-loving perennials which produce flower spikes but are mainly grown for their handsome clumps of big, heart-shaped leaves. There are many variegated hostas, all of them preferring shade.

Their tolerance of shaded, wet areas makes hostas valuable in problem areas of the garden. Popular varieties include *Hosta crispula*, whose deep green leaves are edged with white; *H. fortunei* 'Aureomarginata' (mid green edged

The Japanese angelica tree (Aralia elata) can be a little large for a small garden, but the variegated forms are stunning, especially when the huge flower heads appear in the late summer (right).

The flame nettles (Coleus spp.) are among the most spectacular variegated plants (below) and are excellent subjects for pot plants.

with yellow); and 'Albopicta' (cream, edged and striped along the veins with shades of pale green).

Coleus blumei is a tender annual grown entirely for the leaves, which are brilliantly coloured and variegated in green, yellow, bronze, red, pink, white and purple. They need full sun and, although best as houseplants, some var-ieties can be used in bedding schemes or containers. Pinch out the insignificant flowers to keep the leaves going.

For a really bold statement in a foliage garden, try the su-perb evergreen *Yucca filamen-tosa* 'Variegata'. This gives a dense clump of tall, stiff, spear-like leaves, margined and striped with yellow. In summer it also produces spikes of spectacular white bell-like flowers.

A very similar plant, New Zealand flax *(Phormium tenax)* is available in a large number of interesting varie-ties with different shades of yellow and green leaves and rusty red flowers.

Equally stately are the bam-boos *(Arundinaria spp.)* which resemble giant clumps of grass. The best variegated form for a small garden is *Arundinaria viridistriata*, with green and gold striped lance-shaped leaves. Unlike most bamboos, it does not spread widely.

Herb gardens
Variegated herbs make excel-lent container subjects. They are just as tasty as plain ones, and much more decorative.

For example, the variegated apple mint is considered one of the best-flavoured mints and has white-edged leaves. Similarly, choose a gold and green-leaved thyme, such as *Thymus vulgaris* 'Aureus', and the beautiful gold and green lemon balm, *Melissa officina-lis* 'Aurea'.

Sage comes from a small evergreen shrub, *Salvia offi-cinalis*, which has several pretty variegated forms. They include 'Icterina' (green and gold) and 'Tricolor' (yellow-white tinted pink/ purple).

The splendidly variegated apple mint (above) is, if anything, more tasty than plainer varieties.

The fast-climbing kolomikta vine (Actinidia kolomikta) has small, white, bowl-shaped flowers and remarkable leaves, each randomly splashed with white and pink (left).

VARIEGATED CLIMBERS

There are a host of variegated climbing plants which give attractive dense cover on walls, screens and fences.
● Ivies (*Hedera spp.*). Especially good varieties include *H. canariensis* 'Variegata' (large silver-margined leaves); *H. colchica* 'Sulphur Heart' also known as 'Paddy's Pride' (large heart-shaped leaves splashed yellow); *H. helix* 'Goldheart' (small gold-centred leaves).

Evergreen clinger that does not damage sound walls.
● Jasmine (*Jasminum officinale* 'Variegata'). Deciduous twiner, with scented white flowers.
● Kolomikta vine (*Actinidia kolomikta*). Striking heart-shaped leaves tinted pink and white. Deciduous twiner.
● Honeysuckle (*Lonicera japonica* 'Aureo-reticulata'). Bright green leaves netted golden-yellow. Evergreen twiner.

Index

Index *(continued)*

Picture Credits

Jonathan Aiden: 50 (bottom). Gillian Beckett: 5 (bottom); 9 (top); 28 (bottom); 146 (centre); 148/149 (bottom): 155 (bottom); 157 (top). Julia Bigg/Marshall Cavendish Picture Library: 16/17 (background); 51 (top); 89 (right). Clive Boursnell/Garden Picture Library: 85 (bottom). Pat Brindley: 15 (centre); 16 (top left); 59 (top right); 61 (bottom); 67 (bottom right); 77 (bottom); 79 (bottom); 90 (top); 138 (top and bottom); 170 (bottom). J G Cambridge/NHPA: 99 (bottom). Brian Carter/Garden Picture Library: 5 (top); 19 (bottom); 62 (right); 112/113 (top); 117 (top right); 148 (top left); 153 (bottom right); 161 (top). Colin Carver/Nature Photographers: 73 (top). Collections/Patrick Johns: 17 (centre); 61 (top right); 65 (bottom); 118 (bottom); 122 (bottom). Eric Crichton: 13 (bottom right); 24/25 (top); 27 (top right, bottom left and bottom right); 42 (centre); 43 (top left and bottom right); 50 (top); 53 (centre); 83 (centre right); 84 (top); 97 (top); 99 (top left); 123 (top right); 133 (top); 148 (top right); 149 (top left); 150/151 (bottom); 151 (top right); 158/159 (bottom); 165 (bottom); 166 (top). Stephen Dalton/NHPA: 70 (right); 73 (bottom). Dennis Davis/Garden Picture Library: 112 (bottom). Henk Dijkman/Garden Picture Library: 36 (centre). EWA: 15 (top); 93 (centre); 95 (top right); 96 (top left). Vaughan Fleming/Garden Picture Library: 11 (top right). Geoff de Feu/Nature Photographers: 75 (bottom). Garden Picture Library: 4 (top); 47 (top right). John Glover: 129 (top left). John Glover/Garden Picture Library: 28 (top); 159 (top). Derek Gould: 10/11 (centre); 45 (bottom right); 46/47 (top); 46 (bottom right); 54 (top left); 71 (bottom right); 83 (top right); 83 (left); 85 (top); 90 (bottom left); 120 (bottom left); 121 (top right); 132 (top right); 134 (bottom); 141 (top); 143 (top); 146/147 (top); 149 (top right); 151 (top right); 156 (top left); 160/161 (top). Christopher Grey-Wilson/Nature Photographers: 74 (bottom). Jean Hall/Nature Photographers 60 (right). Marijke Heuff/Garden Picture Library: 12 (bottom left); 19 (top); 37 (bottom); 92 (centre). Neil Holmes: 14 (top); 17 (bottom); 74 (top); 131 (top left and bottom); 132 (bottom); 135 (centre); 154 (bottom right); 169 (centre right); 173 (top). Neil Holmes/Butterstream: 3 (centre), 18 (top), 56/57 (bottom). Hozelock Ltd: 104/105 (top). Insight Picture Library: 48/49 (centre); 92 (top); 102/103 (top); 147 (bottom). Anne Kelley/Garden Picture Library: 51 (bottom). Andrew Lawson: 12/13 (top and bottom); 14/15 (bottom); 16 (bottom); 32 (top left); 37 (top left); 59 (top left); 61 (centre); 63 (top); 64 (left); 68/69/63 (top); 86 (bottom right); 114 (right); 199 (centre); 120/121 (top); 122 (top left); 137 (bottom); 141 (bottom left and bottom right); 143 (top); 146/147 (top); 149 (top right); 151 (top right); 156 (top left); 160/161 (top). Michael Leach/NHPA: 102 (bottom). Marshall Cavendish Picture Library: 16 (top right); 57 (top right); 66 (left – five pictures); 88 (left); 90/91 (top); 101 (bottom); 162 (left); 169 (bottom). Peter McHoy: 24 (bottom right); 39 (top); 41 (top); 44/45 (top); 65 (top left); 66/67 (top); 100/101 (top); 104 (bottom right); 105 (right); 106 (bottom); 108 (centre); 120 (bottom right); 125 (top right); 126 (top left); 126 (bottom left); 136/137 (top); 150 (bottom). Tania Midgeley: 6 (top left); 21 (bottom right); 38 (top); 39 (bottom); 59 (bottom); 86 (bottom); 108/109 (top); 110 (bottom left); 111 (top right and bottom right); 113 (top right); 126/127 (top); 128/129 (top); 139 (top). Walter Murray/NHPA: 71 (centre left). Nature Photographers: 72 (bottom). Jerry Pavia/Garden Picture Library: 1 (centre); 116 (top left). Joanna Pavia/Garden Picture Library: 72 (top right). Photos Horticultural: 6/7 (bottom); 7 (top right); 10 (top right, bottom left and top left); 16 (centre left); 21 (bottom left); 22 (top right); 23 (top right); 25 (bottom); 34 (top and bottom); 35 (top right); 38 (bottom); 40 (bottom); 40/41 (bottom); 56 (top right); 60 (left); 77 (top); 78 (top right and bottom left); 79 (top); 80 (top right); 81 (top and bottom); 87 (bottom); 90 (bottom right); 91 (bottom left); 101 (right); 107 (bottom); 110/111 (top); 112 (top); 116 (bottom right); 117 (bottom left); 121 (bottom left); 123 (right); 124 (left); 125 (centre); 127 (top right, centre right and bottom); 137 (right); 142 (top); 143 (bottom); 147 (top right). Lazlo Pulcas/Garden Picture Library: 33 (bottom). Charles Raymond/Marshall Cavendish Picture Library: 56 (bottom left). Morley Read/Garden Picture Library: 6/7 (centre top); 18/19 (bottom); 30 (left); 31 (bottom); 32 (bottom left); 32/33 (top); 82 (centre). David Russell/Garden Picture Library: 52 (bottom). S & O Matthews: 8 (top); 26 (top: 29 (bottom); 41 (bottom); 45 (top right); 87 (top); 88/89 (top); 133 (bottom); 140 (top); 142 (bottom); 144 (top right); 145 (top); 152 (top); 153 (bottom); 154 (bottom left); 154/155 (top); 156/157 (bottom); 161 (bottom); 162 (right); 163 (centre); 164 (top); 167 (top); 169 (top); 171 (bottom); 172 (bottom). Kenneth Scowen: 17 (top). Michael Shoebridge/Marshall Cavendish Library: 124/125 (centre). J S Sira/Garden Picture Library: 115 (bottom); 167 (centre). Harry Smith Collection: 8 (bottom); 20 (centre); 22 (bottom left); 25 (top right); 29 (top); 40 (top); 43 (bottom left); 47 (bottom left); 52 (top inset and centre); 54/55 (bottom); 55 (top right); 57 (bottom right); 68 (left); 69 (right); 71 (top right); 80 (bottom left); 84 (bottom); 92 (top left); 94 (top); 95 (bottom left); 96 (bottom); 97 (bottom); 98 (centre); 102 (top left); 105 (bottom); 106 (centre right); 106/107 (top); 109 (centre and top right); 115 (top); 116 (top right); 118 (top); 128/129 (top); 129 (top right and bottom); 131 (centre); 136 (top right); 152 (bottom); 165 (top); 170 (top). David Squire: 10 (bottom right); 11 (bottom right); 54 (top right); 55 (top right); 56 (top left); 62 (top left); 63 (bottom); 109 (bottom); 113 (bottom). Paul Sterry/Nature Photographers: 75 (bottom). Brigitte Thomas/Garden Picture Library: 128 (bottom left); 134 (top); 156/157 (top); 158 (top). Perdereau Thomas/Garden Picture Library: 34/35 (top). Don Wildridge: 4 (bottom); 21 (top left and top right); 24 (top); 37 (centre); 58 (right); 130 (centre); 168/169 (centre); 171; 172/173 (top). David Willery/Garden Picture Library: 160/161 (bottom). Steve Wooster/Garden Picture Library: 30 (top right); 94 (bottom).